TRAVEL IMPRESSIONS

The Discovery of Golden Civilizations

~

Lucina Ball Moxley

Thanks for a great reunion in Leland
7/24-27/03

GUILD PRESS OF INDIANA
Indianapolis, Indiana

 Published in the United States by Guild Press of Indiana, Inc., Indianapolis.

Library of Congress
Catalog Card Number
96-78246

ISBN 1-878208-93-4

Manufactured in the United States of America

Designed by Sheila Samson

Contents

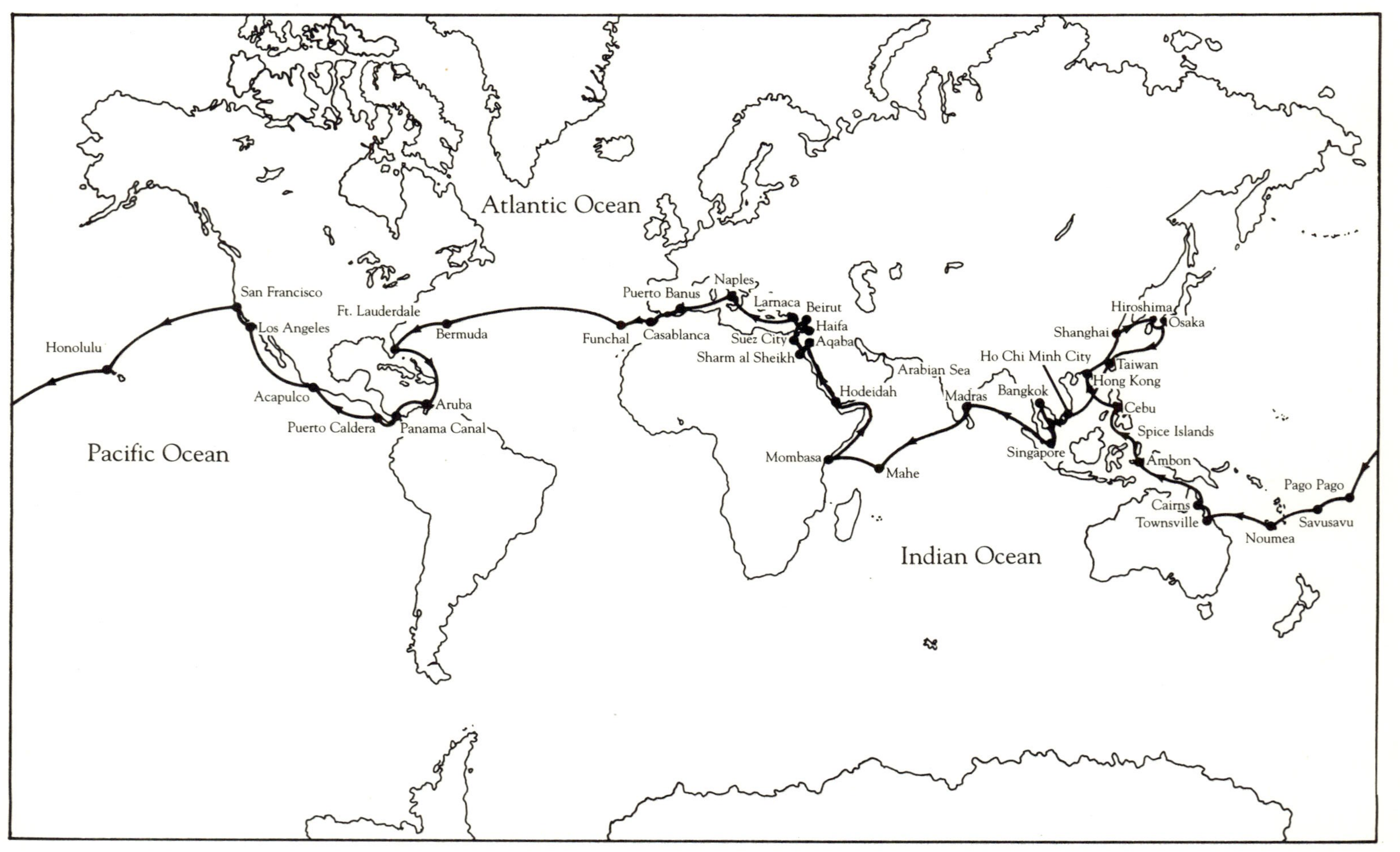
Atlantic Ocean
Pacific Ocean
Indian Ocean
Honolulu
San Francisco
Los Angeles
Acapulco
Puerto Caldera
Panama Canal
Aruba
Ft. Lauderdale
Bermuda
Funchal
Casablanca
Puerto Banus
Naples
Larnaca
Beirut
Haifa
Suez City
Aqaba
Sharm al Sheikh
Hodeidah
Arabian Sea
Mombasa
Mahe
Madras
Bangkok
Ho Chi Minh City
Singapore
Hong Kong
Taiwan
Shanghai
Hiroshima
Osaka
Cebu
Spice Islands
Ambon
Cairns
Townsville
Noumea
Savusavu
Pago Pago

Bon Voyage

~

Pre-cruise Time, and a Blizzard in Indianapolis

January 20, 1996

As I close the suitcases I look through the windows at snow whirling in the wind. Trees coated with ice glitter diamond-like in the sun; an incredible vista of white hills has built up around the acres of my retirement village. I have lived here for seven years, and after two wonderful marriages I now live alone and am free to travel whenever and wherever I like. This time the World Cruise on the *Royal Viking Sun* will really go all the way around and I'm looking forward to this first experience.

There is time to relive good memories and contemplate the cruise to begin today. Will I see the friends that I made on the last trip? Will the cruise be as rewarding as the one last year? Will we sail safely through with no pitfalls?

My thoughts are interrupted by a horn honking in my driveway. The car has arrived to take me to the airport and I am on my way!

❧

As we come down through the clouds for our landing in St. Louis, I am struck by the chiaroscuro of the black and white landscape blocked out beneath us. Black skeleton forests in patches—black roads dividing the fields, lonely black, white, and gray farm houses and dirty snow squares, but not another color to offset the dreariness of the miles moving underneath.

We change planes in St. Louis, then take off for San Francisco.

❧

I look through the wide expanse of windows from my hotel room on the forty-fourth floor of the Mandarin Oriental Hotel and see spectacular San Francisco sprawled below and beyond my field of vision. The night scene is magical. Myriads of light and color pulsate around the contours of high-rise buildings. Christmas every night of the year! Bridges and highways are from this distance streams of light, nose-to-tail; white headlights coming toward me, red taillights going away—somewhere. The bay is a black expanse, dotted with lighted ships tied up at the piers.

Morning light reveals the *Royal Viking Sun* awaiting our arrival in its berth at the foot of Telegraph Hill with Coit Tower perched on its top, a landmark of the city. The *Sun*'s stack is billowing smoke, thick and black. She seems to be saying she's impatient to be off and irritated to be stalled at the stagnant dock.

We don't keep her waiting long. By two P.M. we have been driven to the dock, passed over our credentials and passports, and boarded. The ship feels like home, and I go like a homing pigeon to my stateroom. This is the third cruise on the *Sun* and I've had the same stateroom each time. I like to be on a low deck amidships, because the fare is cheaper and the location is steadier when rough weather hits. I find my luggage already stacked inside, so I quickly unpack my two cases before sailing time. It is unpleasant to unpack if the seas are rough. In a short while slight dizziness can turn to seasickness. Anticipating the usual unsteadiness of a ship, I always take a Dramamine a half-hour before sailing, get settled and unpacked, then go up on deck to watch the exciting sail-off. We push gently away from the dock, glide under the Golden Gate Bridge and immediately begin to roll slightly as the harbor meets the Pacific head-on. With a blast of the ship's funnel, our ship's way of saying good-by and thanks to the pilot, we are on our way.

The travels of my life have extended around the world. Because I love ships, many trips have been the oceangoing type. I have an aversion to plane travel, in large part because I like to see the country as I go, by car, or years ago, by train. So far I have made fifty-nine journeys by sea on forty-five different ships. Many were liners on the Atlantic, crossing to and from Europe, and many were cruises of a range from ten to over a hundred days.

We used to take cameras with us until my husband, Sam, put his foot down. "No more cameras!" he swore. "I'm not going to spend my vacations looking through a view-finder. I want to see everything and enjoy it without the hassle of dragging all that equipment around."

I had to agree with him. The best pictures we could take couldn't match the quality of even cheap postcards. I preferred to take movies (today it's videos) but Sam was never interested in seeing them more than once.

"It's all in my mind," he claimed. "Why should I see those pictures again?"

So we stopped carrying cameras. Now, without envy, I watch my fellow tourists jump out of the buses, struggle to capture shots at every stop, buck high winds, rain or hot sun as they click their shutters and use up miles of film. I'm content to sit "on board" drinking in the views on all sides. Afterwards I record the day's events and feel fortunate to have a good memory.

A camera cannot catch the emotional moment, the catch in your throat as you glimpse a lion with his pride resting in the shade of an acacia tree. A cub is playfully tugging on the ears of the lioness. She responds with a lazy slap of her paw, knocking the cub aside to sprawl at her feet. The lion yawns with boredom.

A camera cannot catch the moment of fear as you watch an elephant lumber across the path in front of your Land Rover. Will he turn to face you and charge?

A camera can't show the ecstasy you feel as you watch a sunset turn into a blazing sky over a Pacific island, the red ball of the sun sinking into the sea at the edge of the horizon. The pictures may be beautiful and reminders of the times, but the excitement is lost in the transition between the shutter and the glossy print.

Impressions of the Sea

My cabin is just one deck above the waterline. This gives me a close look at the ocean as we plow through the water, churning up white froth. Bits and pieces of bright, ice-blue colors are uncovered beneath the foam, but beyond the spume, the ocean's hue is blue-black as far as the horizon. It is the power of the wind that creates the unsteadiness of ships. Turbulence driving against the bow or striking the sides causes ships to lose balance, wallow among windblown waves, and strive for stability.

I have great respect for the sea. The strength and mighty power of oceans is awesome. I have been through hurricanes—one not too long ago when I was certain we would capsize. That experience made me aware of the terrifying possibility of a disaster at sea. From experiences like that I have learned to take life boat drills seriously.

One can't help thinking about disasters on an ocean voyage. How many ships lie on the ocean floor rotting to ruins? Shipwrecks from storms, ships sunk during wars or by adventurous seamen too careless in handling their crafts—many ships have ended up in the depths of the oceans. Not only small ships are victims. Huge ocean vessels can be caught in treacherous storms or collide with other ships, icebergs, or reefs. I recall the disasters of the *Leviathan*, *Titanic*, and *Andrea Doria*.

The great Pacific, so named because of its usually calm character, can rise in rebellion. Storms, hurricanes, and freak waves are almost as common as in the Atlantic. Certain bodies of water, such as the Tasman Sea between New Zealand and Australia, and our own coastal waters of Cape Hatteras, are renowned as violently rough much of the time.

Because the sea changes colors constantly it is fascinating to watch. Sometimes a deep marine blue or an intense green with shades in between, it creates a color palette that would challenge any artist. Then there are the inhabitants below, a whole universe of life strange and unreal, with tentacles, fins, shells—swimming into caves, attaching to colonies of coral, carrying on their life cycles unknown to humans. What mysteries lie beneath the sea—mysteries which have gone on for 600 million years of earth time! Only within the last part of this century has research been able to uncover some of the secrets—discoveries owed to courageous deep sea divers.

A phenomenon I'll never forget was the experience of sailing across the Sea of Oman and getting caught in the doldrums. Just as Coleridge's ancient mariner lay becalmed on his ship for days on end, we idled for a week on a sea that looked like a bowl of jello. On the total expanse far and wide there was not a ripple of air to move the water. The feeling was eerie, mysterious. I visualized a sailor's panic with sails hanging limp, fresh water growing scarce and death close at hand—unless a wind arose to move them on. Mercifully we had engines enabling us to move through it. But the mood was strange, unreal. Like an ancient castle, the sea has many chambers, many moods.

The Discovery of Golden Civilizations

This year we are sailing on a sunny, mild day which contrasts with the heavy rain, fog, and general gloom of the year before. At that time in 1995, the tempest that followed for a week was the worst recorded in thirty-five years, since 1961. I know the truth of that, for Sam and I were cruising in the North Pacific then, our ship battling the seventy-five to ninety mile-an-hour winds and forty-foot waves from Honolulu to Yokohama. We had two weeks of pitching until we received an SOS to go to the aid of a crew on a sinking Greek freighter. That story is recounted in my autobiography (*The Best Years*, Guild Press of Indiana, 1986). Those tempestuous conditions were the same last year, until we reached Honolulu a day late, battered by the heavy seas.

I remember watching the great walls of water rising up against my cabin windows, higher than my eye level, then crashing down to disappear into the sea with furious roars. It was exciting and I was not afraid.

January 26

The sailing has been smooth these first four days with beautiful blue skies and sea, a warming sun, and brisk air, not warm enough to swim but bright enough to redden faces. I am now well into a routine. Always up early, I go to the Garden Restaurant on the eleventh deck for the six o'clock breakfast. This is one time I use the elevator because my cabin is on Pacific Deck number five. Otherwise I climb the stairs, three decks at a time, fifty-four steps. Walking down the six flights is a cinch. It's one way of staying fit on a ship where there are many temptations to be a "deck-chair potato" and eat too much of the sumptuous buffets.

After breakfast of lots of fruit, a piece of toast or muffin and coffee, I go down two flights to the gym where I "work out" for half an hour, bicycling, using weights, and doing general calisthenics. After exercise there is a space of time to write, read, sew on a piece of crewel, or type up my scribbles on this voyage.

Because I have made my career in music, from nine to ten I try to practice on the piano in the Venezia Restaurant, which is usually closed until dinner time. I haven't been too lucky because the entertainers also practice there. If the piano is being used, I go to the bridge lecture, which I enjoy in any case. The couple who give it, Bette and Irwin Politziner, are excellent teachers and directors of the afternoon duplicate bridge sessions. I play every day.

I have lunch in the Garden Restaurant as well as breakfast, because it is bright and airy with picture windows overlooking a constantly changing scene. I go to the dining room where the atmosphere is more formal for dinner. The lunch buffet is enormous—so many choices and varieties of hot and cold dishes. Soups, salads, ethnic offerings of all kinds—and the tempting array of desserts is overwhelming. It is hard to decide but the trend is to just go for it. Mix and match? Tacos with Caesar salad? Take chances! This is the time of day when I am hungry, so I tend to overdo.

From two to four is the duplicate bridge game and I play with one partner or another. We like to switch once in a while and try our luck with someone else. We are an enthusiastic, aggressive bunch and generally have twelve to thirteen tables. This crowds the room but no one minds.

After the games I either go to an exercise class or return to my stateroom to rest and read. I listen to the classical music on the television set, write cards, or scribble on this journal. But I do not enter the lounge where tea is served and bingo is played, because cakes and sandwiches are far too tempting. Fitness aboard ship takes a modicum of discipline.

Formal nights are two or three times a week. There always seems to be a cocktail party preceding dinner and I am invited to many of them. There are also the captain's parties, such as skald cocktail parties on Norwegian night and the welcome and farewell gatherings before dinner. The only casual nights are those when we are in port. I am grateful for slacks and shirt time, for after exploring those ports on foot or on bus tours, I look like a bedraggled sheep caught in the rain. The heat and humidity is debilitating and all I want to do after the day's outing is to eat quickly and escape to my cabin. There is entertainment every night after dinner as well as a movie, but I don't always attend.

Sometimes I'll have a cocktail with friends and dance before dinner. There are several hosts whose duty it is to dance with the single ladies. My feeling about this is rather ambivalent. I realize the importance of having dance hosts and they are attractive and genial fellows, but I prefer to dance with someone who really wants to dance with me and doesn't consider it an obligation. This is a time when I miss Sam so much. He loved to dance and I loved to dance with him. I feel such a sadness when I hear the music we loved to dance to and he is not with me to share it. How unusual and blessed in life to have had not just one wonderful mate but two!

Dinners become long social hours. I sit at the first engineer's table, a table for eight. Rolfe, our host, is a tall, heavyset Norwegian, attractive in a rugged way and comfortable to be with. Another couple, Gerda and George Koraly, and I will make the entire world cruise at this table, but at each leg of the journey some at our table will leave the ship and others joining the cruise will take their places. Gerda and George are Hungarian Americans and we have become good friends. We often lunch together on the top deck in the Garden Restaurant and we also play bridge. They play well and win often. We have this passion for bridge in common and sometimes discuss the hands we have played that afternoon and compare notes and our scores. I have found that this game is a wonderful way to create friendships, and it is well worth learning its complicated systems.

The South Pacific

~

Honolulu, Hawaii

January 27

Slipping silently along the dark coastline of Oahu we approach Diamond Head around the tip of the shadowy hills. Further on, the configuration of lights winding up and into the hills form streamers like loops of tinsel on a Christmas tree. Presently the lightening sky shows a clearer outline of the land, with thousands of twinkling lights skirting the shoreline. As daylight brings out more detail, the magic of the night disappears. Reality gives a truer picture: oil tanks, barracks buildings, and warehouses with scrub vegetation line the shore. Sheds and machinery are piled up in lots, rusting. Cars busily maneuvering in purposeful lines whip along to their destinations in both directions.

My sole reason for going ashore is to put a lei on the grave of Ed Eckerson, my first husband, who is buried at Punch Bowl Cemetery. The ship's shuttle bus runs throughout the day, stopping at the A La Moana Shopping Center, the Waikiki Hotel, and back to the ship on half-hour schedules. After buying a pretty lei from a portly Hawaiian lady at the foot of the escalator descending from the port building I take the first shuttle at nine A.M. From the shopping center I take a taxi to Punch Bowl. It is not far, but it's a twenty-five-dollar fare to go and return.

Ed lies between two shady trees at the drive's edge, not too far from the entrance. After fifty years, his flat, stone marker has darkened from a stark white slab to a mottled gray, weathered and worn.

I cannot stay long. The taxi driver is impatient to return to the shopping center where more fares await. And what more can I do but put the bright flowers down across his name, greet him silently with a prayer and climb back into the taxi? There I dissolve, useless tears flowing as my thoughts, as fresh as yesterday, go back fifty-one years to April 28, 1945, when a Japanese kamikaze pilot deliberately dove his plane into the brightly lit hospital ship—alone and on its way from Okinawa to Guam with one thousand patients.

What price glory? What a price to pay! Lives lost in untold numbers for what? Peace lasts a mere twenty years before another generation has the privilege of dying in another conflict. On and on throughout history it goes. Honor and dishonor fighting to win, this or that cause the reason to attack or defend. The game has been played since the beginning of time and nobody wins in the long run. Humanity has been destined to be the victim of greed, aggression, hate and thirst for superpower status. It's the "little men" who pay the price, while dictators give out the orders, then sit back and watch the spectacle of carnage.

Winners or losers, nations become destitute, decimated by loss of life and property, disillusioned, struggling to regain economic stability, which is more and more difficult to achieve after each war. Why philosophize? Wars will continue even though little people like me argue against conflict. Our fathers, husbands, sons, grandsons, and great-grandsons will eventually be caught up again to fight for "glory." I should add that it will also be our mothers, daughters, granddaughters, and great-granddaughters who will suffer and be killed too. Thankfully my two daughters have been spared the involvement in a war but their lives as well as mine were changed abruptly that day in 1945. Our daughters were the inheritance Ed gave to me, and they were two blessings I had for such a loss in World War II.

Bitterly I watch the scene in my mind from the taxi window. I can't forget the dastardly deeds, the atrocities, the useless killings, the acts done against humanity. Has God excused the wars, the deeds, the miseries? I believe retribution must come to all who advocate violence and the great crime of war.

I release the taxi at the shopping center, buy stamps at the post office, pick up some postcards, and sit in the sunny arcade to fill them out. After mailing the cards I take the shuttle back to the ship. No interest in shopping this time.

I practice for an hour at the piano in the restaurant. At the left of the piano bench a gorgeous view of the harbor spreads out before my eyes. It is a sight to inspire music-making, especially when the ocean is laid at my feet, the sun sparkling silver on the water. I greet the vista with arpeggios and a Debussy prelude.

Pago Pago, Samoa

February 1

The harbor is concealed until the ship maneuvers in and around the opening, turning silently, twisting and heading into the quiet harbor to reveal a passage toward the town of Pago Pago, a view of churches and houses standing out against the jungle green of the hillsides. The harbor basin is filled with bobbing sailboats at anchor, and as we approach our docksite, we see a long line of colorful merchandise hung up, displayed in hopeful anticipation of a big sellout. Salesmen have chosen the shadiest spot to spend the long hot day, guarding their wares under the overhanging roof of a large warehouse. Handcrafted woven baskets abound, along with silk-screened sarongs and lava-lavas, blouses, shirts, and dresses in vivid colors and patterns, shell jewelry, and carved totems. One always has to think twice about buying the tropical, wildly colored clothes. They seem to fit an island setting, but I wonder, How will it look in Indianapolis? This thought stops me just in time.

Passengers gingerly descend the gangplank and are immediately stunned by a blast of heat overriding the frigidity of the air-conditioned ship. We "case-out" the goods displayed, then hurry to the old-fashioned buses lined up for the tours. The buses have been gaily garlanded, with stalks of red ginger lining the brightly painted exteriors. The vehicles are painted in the brightest of blues, reds, yellows, and greens, and are shiny clean to welcome us. The fact that the ancient buses are just souped-up rattletraps seems immaterial. There is a *joie de vivre*, a carnival-like atmosphere surrounding them and their drivers. The "air conditioning" comes from the open window, which circulates as our bus chugs stubbornly up and down the mountain roads, taking its half of the road in the middle. Our guide explains with pride that the drivers are the owners of their vehicles, and we clap with enthusiasm for him and his handpainted decor and flower bedecked interior. "Stained glass" windows—purple isinglass ovals are inset on each side behind the driver's seat, and yellow "glass" triangles adorn the space over the windshield.

The pretty Samoan guide in her brown and yellow sarong-like uniform, with a hibiscus blossom over her right ear, explains that Des, the driver, "antiqued" the plywood paneling of the interior. It was probably done with a wood-burning tool. We are suitably impressed. The erect benches lined up on either side of the aisle each seat two uncomfortably, and sliding glass windows allow the wind to blow our hats off.

Samoan men can be enormous, with huge hams for arms, flat feet like barges and stomachs like those of sumo wrestlers. These men, nevertheless, are often soft-spoken and gentle, and our driver is this type of man. The gentle people have little to offer but what they can make with their hands, yet that is considerable when it comes to crafts. Tapa cloths and wood bowls, silk-screening materials and basket weaving are expertly done. The Samoans seem content with their beautiful island, even though it's often drenched in "liquid sunshine" and subject to cyclones.

Five rusty Korean freighters lie in the bay close to shore where they were blown during the hurricane of 1991. They will no doubt still be there on into the next century.

Spaced at intervals all along the shoreline are round concrete pill boxes, relics of World War II when the U.S. Navy was stationed here to protect and defend Samoa. Otherwise, there is little to remind us of that stressful, agonizing time now fifty years behind us.

I always feel a mixture of excitement and regret when the gangplank is pulled up, disconnecting the ship from the land. People gather on the pier to see us off with the usual curiosity and perhaps envy and wanting to also be on board. The ship's funnel explodes with three great blasts of farewell. Will we come again? My visits have accidently happened nearly every twenty years, 1957, 1977, and now 1996. The changes over those years have been dramatic with each visit. Only the lush, high mountains ringing the bay remain the same.

The first time Sam and I came, we were on the *Mariposa*, and our arrival marked the eighth visit made by a cruise ship to Samoa. Pago Pago was then a sleepy village, and the main square was a grassy plot of land where the islanders worked their crafts, mainly tapa cloths and baskets, while sitting on the ground under the shade of a few trees. In 1977, when we arrived on the *Royal Viking Sky*, the town had grown. They even had installed a cable car which stretched over the harbor, connecting two of the tallest mountains. When we sailed, the cab overhead was filled with people watching us depart. As we passed under the cable car we were suddenly deluged with flower petals as baskets of them were emptied over our heads. The deck was covered with flowers. What a send-off it was back then!

This year the cable car is out of service.

I stay on deck watching the diminishing landscape and taking in the grace and beauty of the hills for as long as it lasts. Even the drenching rain that fell on us during the day, sandwiching itself between bright sunlit hours, could not dampen our spirits or slow down our touring or shopping endeavors. But there was no sellout of merchandise on the dock. I watch the Samoans packing up what remains after the ship has pulled away from its moorings. They fill their truck beds with boxes, chairs, tables and racks. I hope they made enough to offset the long hot day in the sun and rain.

❧

Savusavu, Fiji

February 4

Since the cruise began in San Francisco, we have had interesting lectures once or twice every day. So far, the most impressive for me are the ones given by Jean-Michel Cousteau, son of Jacques Cousteau, the famous diver-explorer and inventor of undersea equipment. Jean-Michel is tall and bearded, with eyes of intense penetration. He seems to be looking within himself and at the same time intensely concentrating on everything before him. His lectures are exciting. He shows videos of undersea life that are exquisite and fascinating, with delivery and choice of words expertly done. Even though he has a decided French accent, his command of English is masterful.

He has brought with him a team of divers, three young people. They made a successful dive in Pago Pago about two miles from the ship, while we watched comfortably in the lounge on the large video screens. They spoke to us and described the sea animals they found as they prowled around the coral reefs, and we asked them questions via a radio transmitter. Much of their fantastic technology is credited to Cousteau and is still in an experimental stage.

I am thrilled to have an experience like this. The diver-photographer and the "mermaid" sit at our table in the dining room. They are an attractive and well-educated couple. The tiny girl is delicate, with long, straight, blonde hair streaked from sun exposure. It falls loosely far below her shoulders. Both Holly and Brett are dedicated to their choice of careers and proud to be associated with Cousteau. And who wouldn't be? I have great respect for this man and his commitment, teaching children respect for the world of nature. He is trying to save the world of undersea life from pollution and man's natural inclination to destroy what he doesn't understand.

❧

One would think all tropical islands are alike—green jungle growth and palm trees covering volcanic hills. Perhaps they would be if it were not for the inhabitants, and the difference lies with the people who call each little square of earth their own. Their individual characteristics create the differences in culture, dress, skin tones and language, imbuing the land with many different tones of life. There are similarities, of course. Soft-spoken, friendly, and unsophisticated are the gentle Polynesians—one family in all their islands. More aggressive are the black-skinned Melanesians, such as those who inhabit New Guinea. The Micronesians seem to show a mixture of the black and caramel-colored skin tones of their neighbors, though "neighboring" means perhaps hundreds of miles apart in the vast Pacific. Their crafts come from the materials at hand—wood fibers of pandanus and palmetto, lush vegetation of flowers and plants.

Savusavu, Fiji, sits on a small spit of land jutting out from the twisted tail of Vanua Levu. Heavy rain has fallen overnight and on into morning, a fact to be expected, as we are in the rainy season. The atmosphere is palpable with humidity at 100 percent. I feel as if I'm drinking water with every breath.

We tender to the land from the ship in sturdy boats and climb into rickety buses. Side curtains are hiding the very view we came to see! Conversation is impossible and the information from the guide is lost in the racket of noise from the engine, with loose parts jangling. We bump over dirt roads, winding through the jungle growth of the rain forest. Eventually we arrive at the thatched huts of the Jean-Michel Cousteau's resort hotel. A year ago we were here for an evening barbecue and the resort was under construction. Now the resort is completed and we are pleased to see manicured lawns, carefully landscaped with flowering bougainvillea and orchids growing in profusion. The greeting we receive is more than a welcome, especially since cool drinks of mixed tropical fruits are handed out among cries of "Bola, bola!" (Hello!) from the cheery-faced black Fijians.

The breezy lanai is a relief from the oppressive heat in the bus, and I sink into an oversized soft chair of rattan and sip my drink. The shady veranda looks out onto a large pool, center stage. Beyond the pool and flowering shrubs is the beach with the sea lapping against it.

This beautiful and relaxing spot is hard to leave, but after a ride in the glass-bottomed boat, the rain clouds threaten again and I want to return to the ship before I'm deluged. Transportation is again the rickety bus to the landing dock, then the tender back to the ship in time for lunch.

Seeing the ocean floor through the bottom of the boat was fun. There were great piles of coral almost high enough to scrape the bottom of the boat. A thin, blue starfish lay on the bottom and bright blue and yellow fish darted in and around the staghorn and brain coral. The colors were less intense through the glass bottom, but later the Cousteau diving team gave us another live show as we sat in the Norway Lounge. Then we saw brilliant colors under the sea. The divers explored much the same area as we did. They were two miles from the ship, but the picture and sound was excellent most of the time. Their video camera showed a great deal of red coral and an unusual starfish which clung desperately to its perch on a piece of coral until Holly teased it persistently. It tried to escape her prodding with its many tentacles of red and white and squirmed frantically to be free, but she kept it captive until she had fully shown and described the rare species. Then she gently put the creature back on its perch. We also saw two gorgeous clown fish darting in and out of the sea anemone, the only fish able to hide safely in an anemone without being paralyzed and eaten by it. These adventures brought to us from under the sea by the divers is for me exciting and wonderful. It has been a highlight of the cruise so far.

Noumea, New Caledonia

February 7

As we sail toward Noumea I spot many flying fish on the way, as well as schools of dolphin. They love to flirt with the ships, skipping dangerously near a lunging bow, but always, somehow, escaping contact with it. It is their game and they love the chase. In the South Pacific flying fish are everywhere. When I first saw them years ago I thought they were birds lost at sea. They dip and dive around the ship's bow, surprised by the ship passing over them. They emerge, springing into the air over the water, then disappear into the depths. Flying fish are silver, red, blue, green, purple, or black. Iridescence flashes when they skim the surface of the sea. My eyes strain to find them, sometimes singly or in pairs, sometimes in a school, but always graceful, arcing, shaping. Where do they come from? Where do they go? Like all of us on the ship, they are transients.

The city of Noumea is surprisingly modern. It is a clean city, spreading out from the port into the hills in all directions as far as one can see. It is unlike most Pacific islands, because the architecture is European style in contrast to the somewhat tropically haphazard architecture of other islands. Noumea has wealth based on the nickel mines in the hills, so it has prospered with commerce. There is a strong French influence as the majority of the population is European-French, and, of course, French is the language.

The tour of the island gives me a little "potpourri" of New Caledonia. I see the working nickel mines, the beautiful countryside and homes, but the most interesting part of the tour for me is visiting the fabulous aquarium which has a unique collection of live fluorescent corals and beautiful marine life of the surrounding reefs of New Caledonia.

❧

A Short Visit Down Under

February 9–11

Townsville, Australia, is a first visit for me. I expected hot weather, but not 106 degrees! The tour I have chosen takes us around the city and to Billabong Sanctuary. We travel in a large air-conditioned bus. The guide insists we all troop about at intervals to see the special landmarks, such as the World War II Memorial. This was where thousands of service men gathered for the Battle of the Coral Sea, won after great losses with help from America and immortalized by the Australians because the victory saved their country from Japanese invasion. Coral Sea Day is celebrated every year on April 25.

Each time I step off the bus, perspiration soaks my clothes, so I try to stay on board as long as possible. After a long drive we arrive at the Billabong Sanctuary ("billabong" is an aboriginal word meaning "water hole"). Small kangaroos gather around our feet begging for the grain we have purchased in small brown sacks to feed them. We walk down the brick paths shaded with vegetation, accompanied by the families of kangaroos, curious ducks, geese, and other birds, all hoping for a handout. Some of the kangaroos have heavy pouches filled with their young, and a few of the apron-like pouches are overflowing. Long, stick-like legs of joeys hang out of them grotesquely, the front half burrowed inside like the proverbial ostrich head in the sand. The creatures are comical with their awkward, big flat back legs and dangling little front ones, but their sweet faces and imploring eyes melt your heart. I cannot resist petting them when they nuzzle up against my knees.

The guides lead us to each area where the animals have their habitats—not caged as in zoos, but relatively free to roam. Only the dangerous crocodiles and cassowaries are kept within protective fences. Young koalas are shown to us and we are allowed to pet them, but not hold them. "Cuddling by strangers is stressful to the animals," the guide explained, "and they do not live long if handled."

I recall the thrill I had when I held koalas years ago. The first time was at the Sydney Zoo in 1957, and again in 1978 in the sanctuary near Brisbane. The little creatures clung to my shoulders as if I were a tree. The eucalyptus odor was powerful and their fur was gummy with it. The fur of these koalas today is soft because they are still very young. The guide (her name is Phoebe and she tells us she is from Carmel, Indiana, where I lived for thirty years!) hands out small vials of thick, milky goo so that we can give the koalas their vitamins. They love the stuff and reach for the tubes eagerly. I insert one into a little mouth and press gently on the hypodermic-like plunger. The marsupial drinks as if it were a baby with its bottle.

Our group moves on to watch the feeding of the crocodiles. Here a sturdy wire fence with a protective barbed wire overhang assures us that the crocs can't escape. These beasts are meat eaters and we could be dinner. Two guides (one is Phoebe) enter through a gate in the compound armed only with a long club and a rake such as is used for raking leaves. They stand on the bank surrounded by murky green water. No crocodiles can be seen, but the guides assure us there is a mated pair lurking somewhere beneath the reeds. They beat the water with the leaf rake and after several big splashes, a huge animal lunges out of the water and pulls itself onto the bank, charging the guides. They barely have time to back away. We gasp with surprise and revulsion at the ugly reptile. The guides pull large hunks of meat from a bucket and throw them toward the crocodile. With a gaping mouth it snatches the pieces of meat and downs them in one swallow. "This one is the female," Phoebe informs us. "The male is much bigger."

Phoebe walks to a further bank and begins to beat the water

with her club. The splashing finally arouses the giant male and he springs out of the water with barely a splash, growling in anger. He is monstrous, hideous. Fortunately the bank is too high for his heavy bulk to make it all the way up and he hangs halfway up the bank, his tail still dragging in the muddy water. He snaps at the offered chunk of meat and it is gone in an instant. These animals are fourteen to sixteen feet long and weigh several tons.

I shudder and move on to a friendlier area after the guides are safely out of the enclosure. Friendlier? Well, it's only a bird, but the fence is made of steel and is very high. This is the cassowary's cage, and he has plenty of room to run around. The guide tells us about this bird, which cannot fly and is nearly as large as an ostrich. His feathers are black, but his head is brilliantly iridescent with green, blue, and red feathers. Two limp wattles, red and very wrinkled, hang from his long neck. His sharp beak and beady black eyes look mean. The guide admits he is afraid to enter this cage.

"He chased me around his feeding tree once until I thought he was going to get me. Cassowaries mean to kill you. They're more dangerous than almost any other animal because they are so quick. When they attack they stretch themselves to their full height of eight feet or so, then lunge with their powerful legs. Their three toes have spurs and as they strike, their claws rip down and you're disemboweled in a moment." We listen in awed silence.

"I'll show you how dangerous he is, folks."

The cassowary is pacing restlessly back and forth behind the gate. The guide rattles the gate and instantly the bird slams itself against it, trying to reach the guide. We know now that this is indeed a killer bird.

After a moment the cassowary cools off and backs away. The guide, with only his leaf rake for protection, cautiously enters and fends off the bird as it circles around him. At length the guide makes it to a tree on which he hangs a bucket of fruit. This distracts the bird and he goes for the fruit, snapping at the peaches and grapes.

The bird's attention is not so intent on his food that he disregards the guide completely. Between snatches at the fruit, he eyes the guide, and makes advances. The guide is also alert and waves his leaf rake around, which seems to intimidate the bird. We have been holding our breath anxiously and are relieved when the guide is finally able to exit safely from the compound.

Now we are led to an open piece of ground surrounded by trees. Several guides are there, ornamented with snakes around their necks. They insist that we pet them and have our pictures taken with a snake necklace.

"Perfectly harmless," they keep saying, but I don't fancy having my picture taken dressed up in a python scarf. I decline with a shudder, but several in our group are fascinated. I gather my courage and as the snakes are passed around to be admired I hastily touch one with one finger. Expecting the snake to be as slippery as it looks, I am surprised to feel only dryness.

Phoebe is coming through the trees carrying a wombat. Now this animal is cute! He's like a big, fat teddy bear, and I wish I could take him home. I reach over to pat his plump tummy. Enjoying the feel of his soft, brown fur, I am distressed to see some blood on his black nose.

"Oh, he was probably in a scrap with another wombat," Phoebe explains matter-of-factly. "They do wrestle each other a lot." She mops his nose, unconcerned. He is lying on his back in her arms with legs akimbo, looking helpless, just like a puppy. I am enchanted. At this moment we are told our barbecue lunch is ready.

We follow the guide through the shady paths to a grove set with tables and chairs. Grills are browning chicken, fish, and steaks for an Aussie barbecue. There is a choice of salads, fresh fruit and rolls. Right now I'm more interested in something to drink. I spot another table loaded with large pitchers of orange juice and cool drinks. I am so dehydrated I gulp down three glasses of juice without pause.

It's late when we return to the ship. I strip off my clothes, soggy with perspiration, and take a shower as quickly as I can. I revive under the warm water and recuperate my spirits.

❧

Ambon, Indonesia

February 15

We are the fifth cruise ship to come to Ambon on the small island of Maluku, which is part of the Spice Islands. These were so named by Captain Cook when he explored the south seas and discovered these islands covered with nutmeg, clove, and cinnamon trees. Those spices grew nowhere else on earth until the island group's trees were transplanted to other parts of the world.

We are greeted at the dock with a percussion group and graceful dancers dressed in pink silk sarongs and white lace jackets. As we line up to enter the buses, the guides pin small orchid corsages on our shoulders. "Air conditioning" comes only from the open windows and small fans spinning from the ceiling. The moving bus stirs the air, but as soon as the vehicle stops, the surge of heat is unbearable.

We move along through the town. The streets are littered with vendors selling everything from hub caps to toys. A pile of shoes makes a pyramid on the corner of the sidewalk. People poke through it trying to find a matched pair—a futile exercise, I'm thinking.

We are taken to some sort of market place, a rickety frame building showing windows that are black recesses with no light within. We climb the first of three stories up broken grimy steps, gingerly stepping around a crowd listening to the shouting of one man. I am guessing it is a political rally of some sort. The small recesses that looked so dark from the street are shops, dreary holes with one hanging bulb dimly lighting the interiors. Kitchenware, army supplies, basketry, a man running a sewing machine in his shop and clothes hanging from the ceiling, then stall after stall of fruits, vegetable and spices.

Nothing looks fresh. In fact most of the food looks dusty and decayed. I am anxious to go back to the bus, but the guide tries to entice us up another flight of stairs to see the fish market. I don't need to see it—I can already smell it. The odor of fish is so strong I am determined to leave, but I am afraid to return alone. This building, I am convinced, is ready to fall down. There is also a sinister feel to it, sort of what I imagine the Black Hole of Calcutta would be like. The smell of rotting fish, vegetables, and urine is strong. As we retreat, I notice little puddles lying along the base of the wall.

The labyrinth is behind us and we are in the baking sun once again. The man is still shouting to the crowd gathered around him and I am curious to find out what it is all about. I peer through a gap between two men. Oh, no! He's handling a snake and is allowing it to strike him! Alarmed I turn to the guide who laughs and explains that he is selling a snake anti-venom and illustrating to the crowd that snake bites do him no harm, since he is immunized against the venom by his wonderful potion. I shudder and tell myself privately that these snakes surely have had their venom removed.

The man puts the snake back in its box and lifts the lid of another box, revealing an enormous rattler coiled up, peacefully asleep. The man annoys the snake by shaking a handkerchief over its head, but the snake is sluggish and doesn't want to play. After he repeatedly attempts to rouse the snake, it is finally irritated enough to strike, but returns again to its coiled position. Evidently both man and snake have had enough. He closes the lid over the box and we move on.

At the edge of a small village we pass a beautiful cemetery. The property was donated by the people of Tantui and maintained by the Australian government. The lawn is lush and trimly kept around a monument centered between two curved walls. These impressive walls are engraved with the names of over one thousand Australians, British, Dutch, and Indians killed during the invasion of Ambon, at that time held by the Japanese, who had captured the island during World War II. The graves of our allies are on rising ground beyond a row of ficus trees. Steps lead up to the site. Bougainvillea and yellow-blossomed rain trees shade the lawn.

I cannot bring myself to go up the steps and walk among the graves as the rest of our group does, because I am on the verge of tears. A group of young singers arrange themselves on the steps and sing a beautiful song for us in memory of those killed so far from their own countries and loved ones. I sit on a bench beside the wall of names, listening and weeping as I relive my own memories.

We drive through many small villages, each one much like the other. Small houses sit on bare dirt yards, their roofs of thatch or corrugated tin. Everything looks so poor. Concrete pill boxes line the road at intervals, particularly on the roads along the coast. Bomb craters are evident among the country villages, vegetation now growing inside the saucerlike holes. Time has smoothed over the ravages of war and life goes on.

I can't help reviewing in my mind the events of World War II. How much these people suffered under the domination of the invading Japanese! That any of them survived is a miracle, with so much privation, starvation, and killing having been inflicted upon them. No wonder that even after fifty years the country is struggling to overcome its poverty.

As we drive along my thoughts return to the present and I am aware that we have arrived at a sort of park on a beach. We wander into an open, roofed building and find tables laid with platters of the local fruit and a punch made of sago. This is rather delicious and has the consistency of tapioca. I taste a little of the breadfruit and a small banana that is hard and dry.

Local dancers perform for us. The dance formations are very much like our western square dances, but I am not too impressed with their amateurish efforts and want to return to the ship. The day has been long and the heat oppressive and my thoughts have depressed me. The tourist business in Ambon has a long way to go.

❧

Cebu, Philippines

February 18

We're coming in to dock at Cebu. The harbor is full of freighters and excursion boats. Outriggers cluster curiously near our ship. I count eight of them from my cabin window. Last night at dinner, Rolfe, our engineer host, said that there are many Filipinos in the crew and all would be given leave to be with their families. Over four hundred relatives will be allowed to come on board.

Another Cunard ship, *Crystal Symphony*, is sharing the dock with us and we will be permitted to board her for a look around. I hope I'll have time to visit it when I return from the tour of Maclin Island this afternoon.

I leave the ship as soon as the captain gives us permission to go ashore. It is 8:30 A.M. I poke around the many stalls set up along the dock to see what they are selling. Shells and more shells! Well, this is where they are found in abundance, but my shell collection went to my granddaughter Breck, because I have no room for them in my little house.

The band is playing and lovely girls in beautiful Spanish costumes are lining up to dance for us. The P.R. office of Cebu is going all out for the cruise ships.

I find a good seat on the large bus well in advance of our departure. It will be an all-day excursion to Maclin Island. We take off a little early for our drive through the city. Cebu is the largest city in the Philippines next to Manila. It is jammed with traffic, mostly trishaws (three-wheeled vehicles used as taxis). They can hold as many as seven passengers—four inside the cab and three on a bench outside at the rear. The small trishaws vie with the jeepnies, which are old army jeeps left behind after the war and converted to buses. These accommodate passengers inside along two long benches which face each other across a narrow aisle. An open rear end serves as both access and exit. The jeepnies are brightly and fancifully painted, with large print on the sides stating their routes.

The streets are not wide enough for buses as large as ours. We take up almost the whole width and there is no room to turn corners, park or even back up. Our driver pushes his way stubbornly through the crowds honking at the people, trishaws and jeepnies.

The hero of Cebu is Lapu-Lapu, who killed Magellan and his soldiers in 1559 as they attempted to land. Only nine days earlier he had made friends with the natives, colonized the island, and baptized the people who accepted Christianity. He had presented an enormous cross to the people and a doll representing Christ, the Santo Jesus. But on April 27, Magellan and a landing party of soldiers rowed in from their ship and were surprised by an attack from the shore by Lapu-Lapu and his followers. The islanders greatly outnumbered the Portuguese. Magellan and his men were slain in the water before they could reach shore. Weighed down by heavy armor, they were no match for the strong, naked Indians.

A large monument to Magellan and a mural depicting the fatal fracas in the sea stand in a park. At the opposite end of the plaza an impressive statue of Lapu-Lapu faces the sea and dominates the park entrance. Even though almost the entire city of Cebu was demolished in World War II, the gifts of the cross and the Santo Jesus were miraculously saved. The cross stands outside the cathedral, which was also undamaged, and the Santo Jesus, dressed in red cape and gold crown, sits on the altar in the cathedral.

We cross a bridge connecting Cebu to Maclin Island, and immediately the houses appear more prosperous. The slums and congestion of Cebu are left behind. Although today is Sunday and most shops are closed for the day, a guitar factory obligingly opens its door for us. We are shown how the guitars are constructed, the fine woods used, insuring that Philippine instruments are the best. The factory and showroom are swept immaculately clean and we are treated to some impromptu music on fine classical guitars, mandolins, ukuleles, and a bass viol. One of our group buys a mandolin on the spot.

We pause at a shell market and look over the merchandise. Shell candelabra of all shapes and sizes hang in rows fronting the street stalls. Lanterns, curtains, lamp shades, statuettes, jewelry, and fancy dishes—all made of shell. Stall after stall exhibits shellcraft until the effect is overpowering. I buy a nest of capiz shell bowls and resist the efforts of persistent salespersons to buy more. I climb back on the bus out of the heat.

We are too early for lunch, which gives us time to browse the small, select shops in the stunning new Shangri-La Hotel. It's so modern and elegant it looks out of place in its setting near the beach. A large pool is noisily in use by the guest patrons. We sit in the spacious lounge where groups of chairs and couches are arranged for conversation and tea or cocktails. Some of our group head for the large circular bar in the center of the lounge. I relax on a comfortable rattan sofa, talk to friends, and appreciate the fresh, cool breeze drifting over us.

Presently our buffet lunch is ready and we head down a graceful, curved staircase to a large hall and an adjoining ball room. Parquet floors shine under my feet. A string combo is playing "Besa Me Mucho." Suddenly tears sting my eyes. How Sam loved to dance to that piece!

The buffet is delicious. There are many choices of soups, salads, vegetables and desserts. A grill roasts chicken, steaks, and fish. I choose satés and find a seat in the ball room where tables are placed around a stage. A waiter offers us our choice of drink and I choose a white wine, which is surprisingly good.

At the end of our leisurely lunch we are regaled by a group of folk dancers. They begin with dances from ancient rites and continue chronologically to more modern dances, which remind me of the dances of the Ballet Folklorico of Mexico. There is an unusual Muslim dance and another featuring bamboo poles. While two or four men move the poles rhythmically to drum beats, girls step in between and over them, increasing the tempo with more complicated steps until their feet are almost flying. Then the poles are carried on the shoulders of the men after the girls have stepped on them and are lifted up until their heads nearly reach the ceiling. Carried in this way, the girls dance on the poles like tightrope performers. I am enchanted by the charm and grace of the girls in their gorgeous costumes, but the day has been long and I am glad to return to the cool comfort of the ship just before sailing.

The Orient

Hong Kong

February 21

Something happened to the weather after we left Cebu. Spoiled after a month of smooth seas and sunny skies, we are suddenly caught in the neighborhood of a cyclone, which causes thirty-mile-an-hour winds and heavy seas. Rain pelts the ship and the decks are awash—too dangerous to go outside. We rock and roll for three days on the way to Hong Kong and by the time we arrive the temperature has dropped fifty degrees. It now is only 38 degrees—a record low for Hong Kong and we passengers are finding it difficult to adjust to the sudden change. We layer our clothes to provide the warmest outfits and top them off with jackets, hats, scarves, gloves—anything we happen to have with us before leaving the ship.

I feel a cold beginning and a sore throat, so I bundle up and walk into the ocean terminal where we are docked. I'm looking for a pharmacy. It is Sunday and also Chinese New Year, so the hundreds of shops in the terminal are closed. The enormous, vast building is gloomy and deserted, but I find the Omni Hong Kong Hotel down an escalator and a drugstore on its second floor, open for business.

The Chinese pharmacist advises an ancient remedy for my runny nose and scratchy throat. He persuades me to ignore the familiar cold pills and cough syrups. He points to medication covered in Chinese writing with faces of ancient Chinese "Smith Brothers" wearing long beards and mandarin jackets, assuring all comers that these miracle cures have been used for ages. I decide to go for the wonder drugs, pick up a few postcards and pay a whopping thirty dollars for the three items, then hurry back to the ship.

I stay on board the rest of the day and watch the rain falling outside in the bone-chilling, foggy atmosphere. Time is spent doing my laundry, typing up my notes, and practicing for awhile. I love having the ship to myself while my unfortunate other co-passengers are touring in the rain.

My hopes are dashed for warmer weather. The next day continues cold. Thick fog hangs over Hong Kong like a gray blanket and I am facing an all-day tour to Lantau Island. My incipient cold seems to be repressed, so I dress in my warmest clothes, really not adequate. A cotton turtleneck and my big wool Ecuadoran shirt, all stuffed under a windbreaker (a gift from Cunard that would fit an orangutan). Heavy socks and shoes will keep my feet warm, and I pull my little golf hat down. Will it be enough for 38 degree dampness? I grab my plastic raincoat just in case.

As I step off the gangplank, the chill wind from the harbor knifes into me. I pull the raincoat on and follow our group through the terminal and out again to the windy dock where we stand and wait for the Chinese junk to take us to the island. The harbor water is choppy, and the junk crunches against the pilings and heaves up and down against the dock as we gingerly walk over the shaky gangplank. Two strong sailors lift me bodily up and over into the junk. I weave my way to the closest chair—as far as possible from the open drafty doors.

It takes an hour to reach Lantau Island, with the junk rocking and protesting the whole time against the wind and rough water. Boat traffic in Hong Kong harbor is like traffic in Times Square: one expects a collision at any moment. We live in suspense, but eventually we arrive without mishap. A cup of tea en route keeps me from solidifying into a chunk of ice.

A bus is waiting for us and we climb in, expecting warmth

from the heaters. But no. The guide apologizes: "We have air conditioning but no heat in our buses, as we have never needed it." I notice that he is dressed in an Arctic ski jacket and is wearing thick wool gloves.

So we spend five hours in the cold bus sight-seeing around the island in deep fog, stopping for scenic shots of the mists for those with cameras. The fog is heavy and the cold gradually penetrates our very bone marrow. The main objective of this tour is to see the Great Sitting Buddha on the mountain top near a monastery—the tallest sitting Buddha in the world. Of course it is thoroughly obscured from view by the fog. The guide is ever optimistic and prays fervently to the Buddha in the clouds for the fog to lift. Buddha refuses to answer his prayers. By this time we could care less. Our teeth chatter, our breath sends forth clouds to match God's formations, and we huddle miserably into our jackets.

We come to the monastery and wander through empty rooms until we enter a huge, barn-like room seething with Chinese. Round tables are loaded with many bowls of Chinese food, half-eaten. Everyone is shouting. Seeing this plethora of diners, consuming or having consumed the food, gives my stomach a jolt. Is this our dining room? I shudder at the thought, but mercifully we are led through this mass of Chinese confusion to enter another dining room, nearly empty, where we find clean tables. We sit around two large round tables and await our vegetarian monastic food.

Bowls filled with mysterious concoctions are brought to our tables and we try samples of each and ladle them into our small bowls. The food is surprisingly good. Best of all it is hot! I cannot begin to describe the various ways the vegetables were prepared, but the seemingly Spartan lunch is filling and satisfying.

Now is the time to search for a rest room—a glorified name for what is reality. The guide is dismayed to admit it, but he points outdoors to a row of bright blue portalets. I determinedly walk out in the cold drizzle and along the muddy path thinking, Well, any port in the storm. I try one of the blue metal doors and recoil at the sight of the interior. How to manage is the problem. It is unisex—a urinal on one side and Japanese-style toilet across the back. But how to reach it? It is too high to step up on it—"it" being just a hole with places for your feet on either side. I simply am unable to step up that high with no handhold. I'm terrified of slipping and falling on the stinking wet floor. And even if I were to make it, how would I get down? I consider trying the urinal, but of course it also is too high. Things are getting urgent and time is passing as I contemplate the alternative. Hold it or let go? What else can I do? I study the floor., puddly from rain or perhaps others like me who have made such a decision. A little more added can't hurt. Thus, feeling remorseful but blissfully relieved, I scurry out of the portalet and join the others for the walk to the bus.

What a day! It should never have happened. Seven hours in the cold, wet, foggy, dismal weather. I can't wait to get back to the ship, but there's still that hour to go on the junk.

For me the entire aspect of Hong Kong has changed and it isn't because of the weather. When Sam, his mother, and I first visited Hong Kong in 1961 it was a thrill. Entering the gorgeous harbor, we saw exotic sampans by the dozens gathered along the sides of our ship. The excited boys in the boats shouted for coins and dived for them as passengers tossed them overboard. Junks hugged the docks, parked deck-to-deck. We could see the families making their dinners on Mongolian hot pots and sitting around little tables eating, the smoke from the hot pots curling up the brass chimneys from the charcoal embers below.

The sky was red from the rising sun and ferry boats plied to and from Kowloon to Hong Kong Island. In those earlier days all was exciting, and we were eager to explore this beautiful city with its tall buildings and still taller mountains framing the background. There were tenements and plenty of them, with laundry hanging from the window sills and stretching across the streets from one building to another.

There was a lot to do during the festive week of that first visit.

Chinese New Year was to begin four days after our arrival and we were busy shopping before the stores closed down on us. Sam said he was saved from bankruptcy by the holiday, because our shopping spree of tailor-made clothes and shoes would keep us in style for years to come.

The morning Chinese New Year began we were startled awake by explosions shaking the hotel. We jumped out of bed and ran to our tenth floor window and looked down on the street. A crowd had gathered, watching the smoke and crackling explosions climb up the building across from us. A rope of firecrackers hung from the roof to the ground twenty stories below, and it took a half hour for the fireworks to burn themselves up to the roof. What a way to announce the beginning of Chinese New Year! At six A.M. the crowd was shouting and cheering, and this celebration was happening all over the city. Once we knew we weren't being bombed by invaders we joined in the excitement of the celebration. Lion dances in the streets and general merriment prevailed. I learned to say Happy New Year in Chinese—"Kung hei fat choy."

How different it is nowadays. Fireworks are banned as too dangerous. High-rise buildings choke up every possible space around the harbor and rise up on the hills beyond. Harbor traffic is intense, but much of it has been diverted through an underground tunnel connecting Kowloon to Hong Kong Island. In my opinion Hong Kong has lost its charm and character and has grown to a sophisticated impersonal giant of commerce, much like New York City.

Shanghai, China

February 25

Shanghai is a sprawling gray city, colorless until evening shadows bring out the midway-like atmosphere of neon. Sinister undercurrents seem to lurk beneath the more sedate surface of the city. I feel the presence of underworld activity—a city of secrets growing and multiplying unseen like a field of mushrooms. At least four derricks tower above the lower buildings, proving there is much building in progress. This city is competing with Hong Kong—fifty years behind, but rapidly catching up.

Our tour winds around polluted streets and neighborhoods full of laundry hanging on bamboo poles overhead. Busy traffic darts about in all directions. We visit Yu Garden. I know it's lovely most of the time, but now it is grotesquely decorated for Chinese New Year. Gaudy mannequins pose in every nook and cranny. Scenes depicting the ancient fairy tales of their religion fill the rock beds. Plastic flowers covered with plastic bags float in the ponds by the hundreds. The swimming carp haven't a chance of survival trying to avoid the garish fake "water lilies" studded with light bulbs.

The horror of all this phantasmagoria of plaster and plastic seems to delight the Chinese visitors at Yu Garden. The people are out in droves, lending a carnival air to the setting. All in all there are forty scenic views to be seen on the ten acres of land, from pagodas, temples, tea houses, and lakes. This being the year of the rat, Mickey Mouse has not been neglected. Disney creations cloned many times over are prominently displayed. A high stone wall surrounds the property and stone dragons, enormous and impressive, slither atop the old wall. The ivory teeth in their gaping mouths have become badly snaggled over the centuries.

It would be amazing to see Yu Garden at night lit with thousands of lights, but we have to forego that pleasure as our ship sails at sunset. I imagine it would rival Tivoli Gardens in Copenhagen—the most flamboyant park I have ever seen until this, but done in far better taste.

Looking beyond the garish trimmings, one can realize it is a beautiful classical garden, constructed privately by loving hands in 1559, and taking twenty years to complete. This hodgepodge of plaster and plastic looking like Disneyland is a desecration of the beauty and tranquility of an ancient Ming Dynasty art form.

Hiroshima, Japan

February 28

I have no interest in reliving more of World War II in Hiroshima. Sam and I were given a full treatment in 1977 of Peace Park, the museum of horrors and ruins left after the atomic bomb finally stopped the war.

I choose instead a tour that will take me out of the city, the tenth largest in Japan, now grown to immense proportions. Our group is ferried to Miyajima Island, which is an ancient historic shrine and features the famous orange torii gate erected in the sea to guard the entrance to the main shrine. The gate can be seen across the water for miles and is pictured in many a brochure of sights to see in Japan. I remember being here before, but the island is now built up with houses and shops. It hardly looks the same except for the old shrine, the gate, and the deer. Deer roam everywhere, gently begging or resting aloof and disinterested beneath trees. I can't imagine where they find food, as not a blade of grass can be seen anywhere. The ground is of packed dirt with roads and paths leading to the shrine or the village. But the deer look sleek and healthy. I decide that they must be fed by the island inhabitants.

The weather is bitterly cold and my own cold has developed in spite of the Chinese "miracle" drugs. We walk for two hours and finally it is time to meet as a group for the ferry ride back to the city.

It is good to be on the ship again, shivering and ready for a cup of hot tea.

Japan is not my favorite country, for obvious reasons, and at our next port of Osaka I stay on board and nurse my cold. I don't go to dinner, but order a light supper and eat in my cabin.

❧

Taipei, Taiwan

March 4

I want to return to Taipei some day. It is a beautiful, green, mountainous country, and a prosperous one. Friendly people wish to help us strangers, and the traffic is bustling but orderly. We drive to the capital city by bus from the port of Keeling. The guide is bubbling with enthusiasm and promises to unfold the secrets of his culture and reveal some surprises as we speed along. It is a bright spring day—a delight to feel my bones warmed and relaxed after shivering from Hong Kong to Osaka.

The excitement builds as we enter the city, which is dressed in red and yellow. It's the last day of Chinese New Year and the Celebration of One Thousand Lanterns is in full swing. We drive around the main square, which commemorates General Chiang Kai-Shek. Red and yellow lanterns hang in rows from poles and trees in symmetry. The imposing white memorial building in the square's center stands aloof from all the frivolity of the day. Floats filled to the brim with lanterns for sale and display crowd the sidewalks. The lanterns depict everything imaginable in all shapes and sizes and in rainbow hues of bright colors: Lantern princesses in robes of orange, pink, green, and blue; lantern airplanes, cars, ships, bicycles, and balloons. There are lantern Disney characters (including Mickey Mouse, of course, this being the year of the rat), and lanterns depicting fairy tales of the Chinese culture.

Entire classes of children march behind teachers who lead the way to the park. The children are in uniforms of blue and white, brown and yellow, and navy and red, with hats to match. Their faces shine with anticipation, round rosy cheeks pinker than usual from the excitement of the day.

We stroll through the park toward the memorial building, intermingling with the townspeople, children and tourists like ourselves. We gape at the sights and are dizzy with the colors. The air is clear and fresh, and I'm drunk with spring fever.

The memorial building houses memorabilia of Chiang Kai-Shek; a giant statue of him is on the second floor. There are offices, an auditorium, and a newsstand on the main floor.

We leave the park on our buses and arrive in congested traffic to a Buddhist temple swarming with worshippers. Most are carrying handfuls of incense (joss sticks) and intoning prayers wherever they stand. The air is smoggy, thick with the sandalwood incense. Long tables on either side of the courtyard are covered with bowls of fruit—oranges, apples, mangoes, papaya, bananas, and watermelon. The fruit gleams with freshness; flowers are laid among the bowls of fruit—cakes and other foods as well. I'm wondering if this succulent feast will be enjoyed by the crowd and I'm tempted to reach for something myself. But this array is an offering to the Buddha who sits placidly within the temple, a gold blob of fat, looking benignly at his worshippers genuflecting at his feet. "He's eaten too much already," I think as I look at the gross statue.

The temple is dense with bodies. It's almost impossible to move through them and the din of voices rising above it all is a cacophony of sound. Then suddenly, there is beautiful singing on the steps leading to the altar. It seems to be extemporaneous, but the voices are completely in unison with a lovely quality. Hymn-like verses are sung by many voices, mostly women. It is an enchanting musical experience for me, and as I listen I have the impression of this scene in the temple as a sea of red. The temple is red and gold, people are dressed in red or black, red incense sticks and the red flames in the burners receive offerings.

The red of excitement seems to burn through the crowd.

The red of heat crushes against hot moving bodies, flowers, drapes, flags, lanterns. All blend to burn an image of fire in my mind.

We make our way with difficulty through the teeming mob,

passing vendors and beggars, cripples, and children with hands out, pleading. We have been told to pay no attention to anyone begging or selling or we will be deluged with a train of them surrounding us. We climb on our bus, still dazed by the awesome experience.

A Mongolian buffet lunch is offered next in a large, clean and sunny restaurant. We choose what we want to eat from the buffet and the chef grills our meat while we watch. The lunch is delicious. I'm hungry, having been stimulated by all the food laid out in the temple.

After lunch we visit a magnificent museum housing the finest Chinese treasures that exist in the world—some six hundred thousand items crafted of porcelain and bronze, stone carvings, and many other artifacts. These treasures were taken out of China by Chiang Kai-Shek to prevent their destruction during the war. Now China wants the collection back, but Taiwan claims the right of ownership, since the treasures were given to Taiwan for safekeeping.

The museum itself is modern and still under construction. Only two floors have been finished and have exhibits on display. The guide explains they are constantly rotating about two hundred thousand pieces at a time until the museum is completed. It is a staggering sight—too much to see and absorb in a couple of hours. I am particularly impressed with a gallery showing the progress of Asian culture as compared to Western or European culture by wall charts beginning from 6000 B.C. to the present day. Studying the dated charts keeps me fascinated for at least an hour. Chinese culture was far ahead of the Western world. I want to return to Taipei!

Ho Chi Minh City, Vietnam

March 7

I am also eager to return to Vietnam—I found the country fascinating last year, but I'm still fighting the cold and constant coughing, which has developed into bronchitis. I take a morning tour with no stops except for a drink at the Rex Hotel. This had been the U.S. Army headquarters during the Vietnam war.

Last year I took an all day tour to the Cu Chi Tunnels—125 miles of underground tunnels and bunkers where the Vietcong conducted the war from their side. Seeing the tunnels was a chilling experience and one that made me understand the hopelessness of that nine-year war.

We drive through Chinatown and see points of interest, then arrive at a large square where we pause for awhile to see the market.

A milling crowd throngs the central square in old Saigon. Bicycles, trishaws and motor bikes vie with people on foot moving in all directions. In the confusing traffic jam I see beggars, cripples, babies in their mothers' arms, all reaching out in desperation for coins. Others offer cheap articles to sell—postcards, combs, pottery, and a hodgepodge of plastic toys.

My eyes fasten on one young man—I'm guessing no more than thirty. He carries a sack on the stumps of his skeletal arms, because he has no hands. His face is grotesquely disfigured in a perpetual grin showing a row of teeth rearranged to ride down his face on a diagonal. It is plain to see how this boy's body was maimed so tragically.

I visualize a ten-year-old boy venturing into the rice field of his parents—well, it had been a rice field. He must get to work and help his mother prepare the field for sowing. He is all she has now since his father and older brother were killed during the war. Now, at last, the war is over and the bombs have stopped dropping. It is time to get to work. Food is scarce and rice must be planted.

He crosses the road and begins to clean out the rocks and metal pieces tossed over the ground by the explosions.

"Ma tells me to be careful," he is thinking, as he piles the loose stones in a neat pile beside the road.

He catches a glimpse of a large piece of metal as the sun gleams on it and his heart beats hard in fear. He leans down and relief washes over him. "It's not a mine, it's a G.I. helmet!" he cries and stoops to pick up his trophy. As he does a blinding flash of brilliant light and colors and deafening noise wash over him. He loses consciousness.

My imagination is as real as the experience this boy must have endured. He now meanders aimlessly around the square and I watch him, stunned with horror combined with deep sympathy. As he approaches our bus I beckon for him to come to my window. Here is a man who was maimed for life as a child in a war he had no part in—an innocent victim of a political war that was a disgrace to America.

I throw some money in the cloth bag that he carries over the stumps of his arms and turn quickly away so he cannot see my tears.

Bangkok, Thailand

March 10

Bangkok is a city of contrasts and extremes. Next to Jakarta the traffic in Bangkok is the world's most hectic. It is not unusual to be stalled in an eight-lane traffic jam for an hour. The pollution and smog of exhaust fumes hangs in the air, causing pedestrians, policemen and city workers to wear protective face masks. Our tour allows three hours for the drive to Bangkok from the port of Laem Chabang, but it is Sunday when we leave for the overnight stay in the city and the traffic is unusually light. We arrive at the Shangri-La Hotel in just two hours and marvel at the scant number of cars on the roads. It is the day of the funeral of the Royal Princess Mother and most of the population has stayed home to watch the all-day ceremony on TV. Only VIPs are permitted to attend the actual proceedings, but thousands have stationed themselves around the square to watch the procession to the royal crematorium.

I have a few minutes to watch TV in my hotel room as I unpack my overnight things. The colorful procession is in progress, and the great funeral chariot is being drawn by two hundred and sixty-one men in traditional red robes and helmets, which look like crowns of red and gold. The funeral chariot itself looks like a pagoda with gold ornate carvings that rise up in seven tiers to a platform holding the remains of the Royal Princess Mother. Overhead is a high peaked cover that ends in a tall spike and is draped with flowing yellow curtains. They are now pulled back tied at each corner and billow in the breeze as the chariot moves along. A wail of mourning music from a piper signals the start of the ceremony at the Grand Palace Throne Hall. The entourage moves towards the royal crematorium, which is another pagoda-like building. The royal urn is transferred to a three-poled palanquin carried by men in traditional white garb, then to the royal funeral chariot in front of the Wat Chetuphon (Temple of Dreams). Arriving at the crematorium the urn is lifted down from the chariot to the palanquin, then is carried around the crematorium in a counter-clockwise direction three times. The royal family has joined the procession and after the urn is taken to the funeral pyre, the king and queen place sandalwood flowers on the pyre, which His Majesty lights. The heavy scent of sandalwood fills the air as the onlookers clothed in black or white burn incense sticks as offerings. "Farewell to the Princess Mother," is the headline in the paper the next morning. From the newspaper I am able to record more accurately the details of the parade, as my viewing was limited and my understanding of the proceedings even more so.

On my way to lunch I look at the shops in the hotel. We were told that on Sunday the shops would be closed, especially on this Sunday, the day of the royal funeral. But one shop seems to be open, though the salesgirls are glued to the television. They pay little attention to me as I look over the racks of clothes. My eye picks out a silk suit with the exact same pattern I had seen in Ambon made of jackets for the tour guides. I had looked for a blouse of the same pattern, but only found a stole, which I bought in Ambon. Now here is the same thing in Bangkok! I ask the price and it is high, as I expected, so I move on to the terrace for the buffet lunch, still thinking about the suit.

A large buffet is set up on many tables under the flowering trees. I choose chicken and beef satés from the iced display and take them to a chef who grills them as I watch. My appetite is stimulated as the rich scents of curry and beef reach my nostrils. I help myself to the cooked food and dish rice and vegetables onto my plate. I'm careful to spoon below the surface of the dishes to avoid any possible contamination from flies. I haven't really seen any flies, but one never knows. I order a bottle of mineral water and sit in the shade of a large ficus tree to enjoy the exotic lunch. Most of our group have settled in the air-conditioned dining room, but I prefer to lap up the warmth outdoors and the scenic views of the landscaped garden with the long canal drifting along beyond the bank. Outboard motorboats spin by like big, buzzing mosquitoes. I revel in the balmy air after the past week of biting cold. I feel almost well, though my cough still plagues me.

After lunch and with time to spare before rejoining my group, I wander back to the shop to look at the suit once again. I decide to try it on. The jacket fits well, but the skirt is too small.

"We can alter the skirt for you, Madam," says the salesgirl.

"I really could use the jacket," I reply, "but I have no time for alterations."

"If you want the jacket, that will be fine—and it looks very good on you." The girl seals the deal for me with the compliment; and the price has been cut in half, thus tempting me from an economic angle. I buy the jacket, pleased, and decide to wear it tonight for dinner over my white slacks and dark blue shell, which I brought along with my overnight things. The jacket is a rich, dark, wine-red silk with insets of patterned cotton cloth in the full sleeves and back and front panels. The design is a mixture of colors—black, white, dark blue, and green geometric patterns. I love it.

Our tour begins with a visit to a Buddhist temple to see the Great Sitting Buddha made of solid gold and weighing five and a half tons. For two hundred years the gold was hidden under a coat of plaster, hurriedly camouflaged during a war with Burma. Buddha concealed its precious secret until the day when an attempt was made to move the immense idol. In the struggle the Buddha was dropped and some plaster broke off. The gold was discovered underneath and now it sits glowing on an altar in the dim recesses of a dingy temple. We take off our shoes in respect for the deity before walking in to catch a glimpse of the mountain of gold.

Our sight-seeing schedule has been planned to include zero shopping. None at all, until cries of protest burst from the women. The men sit back with smug looks. It is finally agreed that if we finish our tour early, a small bus will take those interested to some shops. Those not wanting to shop will be returned to the hotel. However, those who elect to shop will only have fifteen minutes to wash up for dinner. This alternative is hopeless. I know that by the time the long day is finished I will feel too grubby and exhausted to do anything more. I will end up going back to the hotel for a luxurious foam bath and relax. Besides I already have my purchase!

We drive and drive endlessly over dusty, bumpy roads that reach into the country. The potholes are so deep that progress eventually becomes impossible. After an hour, fearing our bus will lose an axle, we stop abruptly in the middle of nowhere. One-lane traffic and machinery congest the road. A few times we have leaned crazily over on the brink of toppling into ditches. We can go no further and are told we must walk the rest of the way or ride in a minibus that has miraculously materialized and is waiting for the fainthearted beside a dirt lane. Some walk but I ride. The sun is beating down and the narrow lane seems to go on and on. I wonder where in the world we are going that is so important to endure such terrible roads. Truly it has to be a dubious destination.

We come to a gate, which is padlocked. A high wall hides the property beyond. No one answers our calls. We move on to another gate, also locked, but through it we glimpse a man who is reluctant to open up for us. This being Sunday, I'm guessing we've made this trip for nothing. Now another man appears behind the gardener (for that is who he is). He greets us jovially, unlocks the gate and we walk into the "secret garden." We look right and left at indescribable beauty of flowering plants and trees. The jovial man is a tall and robust Thai in his seventies. He leads us to a terrace filled with ancient statuary and pots of flowers. We sit at tables under an arbor and are served welcome glasses of mineral water while our host, Khun Prasart, relates the history of his museum and garden, both of which house his treasures. He has been a collector of fine art for thirty years, with the compulsion to save the ancient Thai culture for future generations, because he believes it is disappearing with the modern age. Gradually his collection grew until he had to find a place for it. The idea of a museum was born. He designed the buildings and landscaped a bare piece of land in the country beyond the city of Bangkok.

Almost single-handedly he tilled the ground, planted trees and shrubs, dug pools and fashioned walkways and bridges through a garden that has bloomed into an Eden. In twenty years the result of his labors are ten acres of land developed into gardens and buildings in the traditional Thai style. There are twenty buildings nestled in among the gardens—four pavilions, two chapels, two residential buildings, a library, bell tower, garden shelter, two museums housing Thai and Western art, a Chinese temple, reception area and souvenir shop. Two ponds enhance the garden and Thai house. Ming statuary has been placed along the paths among the colorful shrubs. The buildings have been constructed using antique portions from the Prasart collection, such as lintels and panels. The old blends with the new, meticulously copied to conform with the ancient style. The floors are of polished teak and we remove our shoes to walk on them.

A pool surrounds the tea house, and we stand on the porch looking down at gold carp swimming peacefully among the blooming lotus. Inside, we view furnishings of ebony and sandalwood. Chairs, tables, couches, and artifacts sit on a Chinese silk carpet. The temple has its Buddha presiding on the altar. Fresh flowers and fruit offerings sit at his feet. The pagoda looks like an Ankor Wat relic. As we stroll along the paths the feeling of peace and tranquility pervading the atmosphere is so palpable it becomes a sensation of holy reverence. I feel love emanating from every leaf, petal, stone and bird on a branch, projected into every leaf, petal and stone from our host, who has accomplished the resurrection of his culture with dedication and purpose. His high ideals will leave his corner of Thai history to the youth of the country, so they will surely revere their heritage.

It is hard to leave this paradise and the man who made it come true. I feel a deep respect for this aging man who still works in his garden along with seventy gardeners. I imagine how costly the enterprise is to support, and I leave with regret because it has been a religious experience for me to be with this man, his garden, and his ageless art. I feel renewed in spirit.

After the grueling hour back to the city I am ready to relax in a hot tub before dinner. The long day has used me up, but the younger and hardier souls have taken off in the minibus to shop.

Our Thai dinner is in a restaurant across the canal, or *klong*, just five minutes away by ferry. Shangri-La Hotel has its own dock. We climb in over the bow of the boat, which is moving restlessly in the rough water. It is a balmy but a windy ride. Lights along the banks of the canal illuminate the famous old Oriental Hotel next door to us. There is an annex to the original building, which is now one hundred years old. Lights create a festive mood up and down the canal. We cross to the opposite bank and are helped out of the shaky craft. We remove our shoes in the vestibule and enter the dining room, already full of diners.

The tables are less than a foot above the floor, but underneath the long tables are trenches. We slide under the table and sit comfortably on the floor bolstered by Thai silk pillows. Our feet dangle below the table in the trench.

The meal is served in large bowls by costumed Thais. They crawl around us on their knees to ladle the food into our small bowls. Mysterious concoctions of fish, beef, vegetables, and rice are served up. Everything is spicy, with adventuresome flavors. A small orchestra plays strange oriental music of the pentatonic scale, which is interesting for a while, but then gets twangy.

As our meal winds to an end, dancers emerge onto the stage in glamorous costumes and headdresses. We are regaled with a long program of Thai dances. The girls scarcely move their feet, but pose with graceful arms and supple hands. Six-inch gold fingernails, applied to each finger, gleam like stilettos as these beauties stretch their hands into impossible positions, bending their fingers perpendicularly to their palms with amazing flexibility. Jeweled headdresses and silk sarongs move exotically to the rhythms and melodies of the five-tone oriental scale.

The evening is finally at an end, and we climb out of the trench, stumble to our feet, put on our shoes, and manage to board the ferry without a casualty. The klong is quite rough.

I am glad to climb into the kingsize bed in my room and read a bit before turning out the light. It has been a long day—a day to remember.

I am up early as usual for breakfast and our group gathers for a morning on the klongs. Boating on the klongs of Bangkok is an experience not easy to forget. It takes two boats to accommodate our fifty-five bodies, and we set off tandem style to explore the canals. It is windy and rough, but the sun is hot. Outboard motorboats skim by us and set us rocking in their wake. Confusion of traffic reigns as boats flip by speeding in all directions. Passing outboards, indifferent to their flying wakes, shower us from time to time. One side of our open boat, across from me, has taken a huge dousing and those people are drenched from head to toe. They laugh and mop off as best they can; eventually the wind will dry their hair and clothes.

The canal narrows and the houses on either side are easier to see. They are built on pilings—stilt houses over the water. Each ramshackle building has its own pier, with steps going down to the water. Most of the houses have boats tied up alongside. We watch the people sitting on their rickety docks doing laundry, washing their hair, brushing their teeth. The water is murky with flotsam and jetsam. We pass a dog busily swimming downstream, looking intent but not distressed. I hope he gets to his destination unharmed. The traffic is buzzing with commercial activity; several boats manned by women in broad-brimmed straw hats move up and down the canal. Their boats are piled high with more hats to sell. Flower vendors pass, crowding other small boats out of their way. Green vegetables piled in neat arrangements adorn the stern of one boat floating by. Sampans blend with the larger boats, taxis, and outboards.

A family is enjoying a swim together, and their child floating in an inner tube is laughing with delight as our wake pushes her against the steps of their dock. She bobs and waves to us as we pass, calling out a greeting.

The morning passes pleasantly. We get a good look at life as it is on the klongs. I'm glad I have come through without getting wet because my chest is still congested and I'm coughing more than ever. I think this morning's excursion has brought on a secondary infection and I don't feel well. We collect our bags, board the buses and begin our return to the ship. On the way we stop at the Intercontinental Hotel for a buffet lunch, then speed back to the *Royal Viking Sun*. It's a welcome sight, white and gleaming, waiting for us.

Singapore

March 14

This is an amazing city, both for growth and progress. I have been to Singapore four times, and each trip I have seen amazing strides forward. On our first visit in 1977 on the *Royal Viking Sky*, we came in to an unimpressive large harbor, scenically flat and unattractive. It was an expansive harbor, however, and many ships lay at anchor, waiting their turns to enter to load and unload cargo. The famous Raffles Hotel had to be visited—we stopped in for the Singapore Slings. We sat in the rather run-down bar, an old fashioned garden room. The slings were watered down like the mint juleps at the Kentucky Derby. We were not impressed with the city and flew to Bangkok for the weekend.

Our next trip was in 1978. We arrived by plane and stayed at the gorgeous Shangri-La Hotel, a garden paradise situated at the edge of the city in a wealthy suburb. We shopped happily and took a tour into Malaysia to see a rubber plantation. We also were taken on a private excursion to see an oil drilling rig offshore, at the time owned by my family company of Ball Corporation. We enjoyed our time in Singapore and found it to be clean and prosperous, ruled by a new dictator calling the shots in a no-nonsense manner. Crimes were severely punished; no street litter allowed, etc. No slap-on-the-wrist admonishments. Penalties even for tossing a cigarette aside kept people in line.

Seventeen years later I saw Singapore again, this time entering the harbor on the *Royal Viking Sun* in 1995. A fantastic skyline of tall high-rise buildings lined the coast, and at dockside a huge terminal had been built full of shops and restaurants. A cable car ran overhead to Sentosa Island where a maritime museum, zoo and aquarium could be seen in beautiful park surroundings. The city had grown immensely in size and economic stature and was the envy of the rest of the world for the strict laws that have virtually eradicated crime.

Today even more high-rises have been built. The city is clean as an eggshell and as busy as a bee hive and there is much to see and do. I decide on a tour to see the royal palace of the Sultan of Johore in Malaysia, or more specifically, one of his three palaces.

We cross over to Malaysia by causeway and pass through immigration with comparative ease. The palace is situated in a large park enhanced by beautiful flowers and trees. Orchids grow in profusion everywhere. The Sultan's rare and valuable furnishings and decorative arts are lavishly displayed in the many rooms of the palace.

After the tour of the palace, we have a Malaysian lunch at the Pan Pacific Hotel.

I finally am able to run my bronchitis to the ground. I started antibiotics when I returned from Bangkok and they have done the job together with the four days at sea to give me the rest I needed after the strenuous tours. The weather is hot as we sail to Madras, India, and the Indian Ocean is as smooth as a glass tabletop.

❧

Right: Escorted by a *Royal Viking Sky* greeter, Lucina and Sam Moxley, accompanied on the cruise by granddaughters Breck Cummings *(left)* and Tracey Strohm, prepare to embark on a North Cape cruise in 1979.

Below: The four travelers relax at dinner in the ship's elegant dining room.

Sam and Lucina in Honolulu, Hawaii, in 1969.

Ed Eckerson's grave at Punch Bowl Cemetery in Honolulu.

Lucina, doing a hula, won a first prize for most authentic costume during her 1957 South Pacific cruise on the Matson Line's *Mariposa*.

India, Africa, and the Arabian Peninsula

Madras, India

March 18

Madras is a sorry place—so poor, so dirty, so overpopulated. Everyone begs for money or pesters you to buy something. Clusters of children mash you, persistently begging and following wherever you go in spite of the guide's harsh words. It's even worse than Bombay.

We drive to fantastic ruins that look like ancient temples, but learn from the guide that they were built as an architectural experiment by a school of temple builders. This was their first attempt in stone carving. Mahabalipuram is forty miles along the coast from Madras. The word means "city of seven pagodas." Magnificent, rock-hewn cave temples and masterful monolithic stone figures dating from the sixth to the ninth centuries are cut into the rocks. There is also a colossal sculptural frieze depicting scenes from the epic *Mahabharata.*

It would have been fascinating to spend a long time admiring the ancient works, but the pestering crowd of boys jumping like locusts makes me seek the security of the bus. I constantly worry about pickpockets, even though I carry no money and wear no jewelry.

We drive on, skirting stray cattle wandering the roads. They have the right-of-way because they are considered deities or reincarnations of your grandmother or some such thing. We have lunch on the bench at a nice hotel, but it is windy and I begin to cough again.

Returning to the city, we are taken to yet another temple, where we are told to remove our shoes. This happens on the street in the middle of traffic, but there is a man who collects our shoes at a little stand. From there we walk barefoot (or in our socks) on scalding hot pavement to enter the temple gate. This is true torture. The stones are so hot in the sun, we hop to any spot of shade. Why this trip was necessary I'll never know, but I am irate finding myself walking shoeless on the filthy streets of Madras.

I am grateful when I can board the ship and leave the misery of the city behind.

It takes six sailing days to cross the Indian Ocean to the Seychelles Islands. I continue to play bridge. On the whole, most of the players are above average and knowledgeable about the many new conventions or willing to try them out with their partners. For a while I played with a Japanese woman who really knew it all and was ready to come down on me if I made the slightest mistake. She cowed me into submission under her severe scrutiny, remembering every hand, every card, every play. Thank goodness she left the ship in Hong Kong!

I play every day, involved with different partners a lot of the time, and in spite of the Japanese woman I enjoy it. I have been on the winning team (sometimes east-west, sometimes north-south) a good share of the time. I feel that coming in even fourth place is not bad when every day we have twelve or thirteen tables. I have been invited to play in the evenings in a foursome, and have mostly won those games. Playing for a tenth, I finished $8.50 ahead in the less than ten games we played. I think I can hold my own with either aggressive players or those who are masters and enjoy the game whether I win or lose. I have become friends with quite a few of the regular players, having met them last year on the World Cruise, and here they are again! Bridge is a wonderful way to make friends aboard ship.

❧

Mahé, Seychelles

March 24

I have looked forward to being in Mahé again and here we are! A more beautiful group of islands cannot be found anywhere. The weather is consistently ideal as well. I loved Mahé when we were only here for a short weekend in 1980. It's reminiscent of St. Thomas in many ways, with the mountainous terrain, houses perched on the slopes, and gorgeous views wherever you look. The black population live much like the blacks on St. Thomas and there is little poverty. Driving is on the left hand side of the road, as it is in St. Thomas. The difference is that the Seychelles are much bigger than the Virgin Islands.

Sadly, we are here on a Sunday and the shops in town are closed. But shops are set up on the dock and I browse over the merchandise, finding the prices much higher than what we have been accustomed to on this voyage. I haggle the price down on a pair of slacks and buy them for half price.

I take a ride on a semi-submersible craft to see the underwater life. It is fun to see schools of tropical fish scooting in and out of the coral reefs. Black and white zebras, yellow darting fish, parrot fish brilliantly colored, and bright blue demoiselles delight our eyes. The guide brought along loaves of bread to lure the fish to our boat, but they know we are coming anyway and swarm around, anticipating the bits of bread that will be cast upon the water. We end our half-hour of viewing below and go up on deck where bread is distributed. We toss pieces overboard and watch the fish scramble to snatch the first bites.

Mahé is lovely, with extravagantly beautiful sunsets. It is another place I want to revisit.

During our voyage we have had two unusual experiences. A new comet was seen by a Japanese astronomer on January 31. He called it by his name, Hyakutake. One of our Japanese passengers brought the new comet to our captain's attention and since then "sky watch" has been out on the bridge. On March 26 (my daughter Judy's birthday) we were called to watch the comet from the top deck of the *Sun*. It was about one A.M. A group of us passengers struggled into windbreakers and scarves to meet on the top deck. The captain doused all the lights so that we would be able to see the stars clearly. It was partially cloudy, but as the clouds parted we were able to find the Big Dipper and I'm fairly sure I spotted the comet, though the tail of it was turned in a direction away from us. It looked like just another bright star. In any case, the experience was fun. We thought a better night to see it might turn up, but the sky continued to be too cloudy from then on.

A total eclipse of the moon also occurred, and I wanted to see it, but though I woke up at one A.M. the moon was too high to see from my cabin window. I was too tired to dress and go up on deck. The next thing I knew it was 5:30 A.M. and the full moonlight was falling on my face as I slept. The eclipse started at 1:15 and lasted for three hours. I had missed it all.

Mombasa, Kenya

March 28

Judy's birthday is past and I failed to find her at home when I called. I could only wish her a happy birthday on her answering machine. This was a disappointment. Another disappointment was that I had prepaid a tour for a day safari to Tsavo National Park, but now I am told it would be rare to see animals in the middle of the day. The hard, dusty, three-hour drive to Tsavo would put us there about 11 A.M. We would only be there until two P.M. and then drive back to the ship—another three hours. I felt the trip might be a wasted effort, so I exchanged my safari trip for a day on an Arabian *dhow*. It turned out that I have had a grand adventure on the dhow sailing vessel.

We drive a long way over tacky roads through the tacky town of Mombasa and eventually come to a marineland where a dhow is tied up at the pier. We don't board right away, but climb some steps up a hill to a small village. We are welcomed by the dhow captain and served cups of tea. The captain is a grossly fat German bursting through the tight buttons of his almost white shirt and shorts. He greets us effusively and explains the locations of the rest rooms to those interested (I think we all are).

There are some huts scattered about containing articles for sale and a great deal of beadwork is laid on the ground over bright cloths. The vendors cry out for us to see their wares. Besides beaded jewelry there are many wood carvings, straw bags and the usual handcrafted articles. I start bargaining for a necklace of wooden animals mixed with beads when a tall, handsome Masai warrior magically appears at my side. He is naked to the waist except for many beaded necklaces and a headband that drapes around his ears. Arm and leg bracelets and a red pareu give him a commanding air—not to mention the tall spear he carries. He makes sure that I pay full price for the necklace, beaded choker, and bracelet—and I part with twenty-two dollars. I am intimidated to the core! I mumble to myself as I walk away, "Well, they do have to make a living."

We are called to attention by our German host. "Achtung! Ve go to boat now!" So we march down the steps and board the famous dhow. There are forty of us and the boat is really more of a barge. My imagination had created something like a pirate ship because when we were in the Seychelles, the Sultan of Oman sailed in on his dhow and tied up behind us at the dock. It was a magnificent, three-masted sailing vessel made of rich teak with gold trim around the square portholes, a stunning tall figurehead of gold, and the bowed stern was carved and inlaid with gold. Well, I didn't expect us to rate such an elaborate vessel as that, but I am rather disappointed to see the wide, flat craft—forty-eight feet long with nothing but bench seats lining the sides and stern of the boat. It isn't all that clean either, and looks well used over a great number of years.

Our barefoot beerbelly captain is at the helm and romance has gone overboard. We motor out of the canal with the water rough and the wind strong. We are introduced to the six-boy crew, naked except for their wraparound skirts. They join as a group to sing us a few songs. A basket of bananas is passed around with wedges of lime between the pieces of fruit. The captain assures us bananas are a sure prevention of seasickness. I never thought to take a Dramamine with me. There is a pile of coconuts on the deck by the mast and the crew begins to slice and peel the hides of the coconuts with sharp machetes. They chop the ends off, stick in straws and pass them around. The coconut water is cold and delicious.

The wind and waves kick up impudently and our boat rocks and plunges. It isn't long before one of our group is leaning over the side and some of us begin to wonder if seasickness will strike the rest. I feel fine and try to enjoy the ship's surges. Finally after an hour, the captain cuts the motor and the crew gathers around the lines tying up the sail, which is wrapped around a tall spar. They heave, sing, and shout "hallelujah" with each pull. Suddenly the sail is free and snaps open. We are sailing. The effect on the boat is suddenly calming. The sail itself is a dirty piece of canvas, but it looks brave filled with wind. We have sailed out with the motor, now we are returning under sail. Our seasick passenger is pale but improved.

We are back at the dock in time for lunch with extra time for poking into the shops. (I'm a sucker for wood carvings.) There is also some entertainment. We find benches partly in the shade and watch the Masai warriors in full regalia and spears dance for us.

Rather, it is less dance and more hop. They take turns jumping and hopping, trying to outdo the others. Pretty soon their black skins shine as if they have been oiled. The heat is overpowering in the sun and the men glisten from their exertions. The entire village takes part in the ceremony. Even the tiny boys, not more than three years old, are dressed in Masai garb and proudly carry their small spears. They are adorable. The women stand apart, looking on, holding their babies.

Lunch is served on an open terrace overlooking the canal. Smiling African women pass bread in woven baskets and serve the meat and vegetables from large platters. I'm careful to avoid the salad, but everything that is cooked tastes good. Several people at our table eat nothing at all. They just drink beer.

We have another sail this afternoon, this time through the mangroves in calm water. A dozen extra passengers have been added to our group—eight or ten Africans, two of them women. The men are dressed in red skirts tightly fastened around their waists with the women wearing colorful dresses and turbans around their heads. The men perform for us with fancy acrobatics. They build pyramids of their bodies and do the limbo under bars of fire. They are as good as Chinese acrobats. While they perform, the girls are busy plaiting colored strings in the hair of both men and women in our group. They are creating "pigtails" of purple, pink and orange wool trimmed with beads at the ends. On impulse I beckon one of the girls and offer my head for a "hairdo." She sits behind me and begins at my scalp to braid an orange strand of wool into my hair while I help by holding the rest of my hair up and out of her way as she works. The result is an ornament hanging from my head—two six-inch tails firmly attached in my hair in colors of orange and purple. Three beads of green and black finish off the ends. I am now stuck with this adornment for as long as I wish until I decide to cut the tails off at the base of my scalp! I can even wash my hair and they will remain intact. What fun! After a week I've become quite attached to them, as they are to me. They seem to blend with my clothes and add a certain devil-may-care look to my appearance. The strings fall forward or back at will. A couple of times when I wear evening clothes, I have simply tucked them under my collar and they aren't seen. They don't seem to go with sequins! I'm sorry I missed seeing the animals on the safari, of which I learned were many, but the dhow adventure was fun.

❧

Hodeidah, Yemen

April 2

Here we are in Yemen, a country only recently opened to tourists. The port is just a huge expanse of concrete stacked with containers (like railroad cars) to be shipped out. Men are lazing about, curious to see our elegant, big ship dock. Two men, a large basket between them, walk along the pier picking up trash as they go. Each man holds one handle of the basket and by the time they pass my cabin window the basket is almost overflowing with paper and plastic.

The men wear red and white or black and white checked prayer shawls called *keffiyehs* over their shoulders or wrapped as turbans around their heads. Long wraparound skirts are held up by wide decorative belts, which in turn holds a wicked curved dagger, or *jimbiya*, in a fancy sheath. I see all this from my window as we ease against the dock, and it is not long before the captain gives us permission to leave the ship.

I go with the crowd to find our bus. A seat is vacant behind the driver and I share it with Lloyd Tinkle, one of my new-found friends. This will be an all day trip into the country to a village on a mountain top called Manakha.

The guide and driver are equipped with fancy daggers plunged into wide belts embroidered with gold. They look like pirates.

We drive through a veritable desert for over an hour—no vegetation, trees or grass—just an endless stretch of orangy dirt. In the distance we begin to see the ghostly gray shapes of mountains. As we come closer the mountains loom high and we begin to climb. The terrain has changed and is more and more rugged as we wind around the mountains, making hairpin turns one after another. Eventually we will climb from sea level to over eight thousand feet. We pass through a few wadis where rivers flow and green fields full of crops are tended by farmers who live in straw houses. The huts are crude mounds like piled-up hay bales on an Indiana field. We stop to take pictures of one village and the people come out of their huts, as curious to see us as we are to see them. They are dressed in colorful clothes like gypsies and seem to be of a sect other than Islam, because the women are not hidden under black robes as are Islam women. We have seen very few women at all, in fact. This is definitely a man's world.

After three hours of hard driving we finally reach the summit, the ancient mountain town of Manakha. The houses have changed from straw to stone as we have climbed upwards. Villages or just solitary houses are perched on pinnacles, seemingly inaccessible from any road or path to reach them. The houses are square in shape, built of stone slabs with a door but no windows. There are geometric lines painted on the stone in colors of white or yellow—like a whitewash. Perhaps this is to identify the houses. Otherwise they would all look alike.

Here is a stone city balancing itself on a mountain top, an incredible sight unlike any other. We stop on the main street and leave our buses, which can go no further, to change to four-wheel-drive vehicles. Seven ride in each van, on impossible dirt roads filled with loose stone and potholes. We struggle up one narrow road after another, snaking around the mountain passes. The rough ride creates a certain discomfort in all of us, but here in these parts there is no comfort station. By the time our parade of cars reaches the top there is not one of us who isn't pleading "where can we go?" Unfortunately we have left all rest rooms back in Manakha and must return there for this pleasure.

I am very short of breath in this altitude of over eight thousand feet—in fact we are all huffing and puffing. To see the six-hundred-year-old mausoleum, which is the object of all this struggle, we have to climb higher still by foot. The cars have brought us as far as they can. I climb about halfway up steep steps, then decide it's not worth the effort. Most of us turn back and find where our cars are parked, but it seems miles away as we pant our way along, stumbling over rocks as we go.

We are finally packed into the cars and are on our way back to Manakha—none too soon as we are now anxiously awaiting that "comfort station" down the hill and an hour away. We have been on the roads already five hours since we left the ship and by this time our limit has been stretched to capacity.

At last we are back in town. The drive has been incredible, the scenery fantastic, but we lose no time finding our chosen destination. We enter a building, said to be a hotel, but I see no evidence that it is one. The ground floor is a grubby room set with tables and there are men eating. We are shown a staircase leading upstairs, which is so dark I have to feel my way up. At the top are several washrooms and we hurriedly take turns. We discover the toilets are non-flushable. So what else is new?

There are several rooms on this floor and I choose one to enter. There will be twenty-five of us in each of the rooms. The "table" is the floor, set with a long rectangular cloth. At the edges of the cloth are paper plates and bottles of water, much too close together to accommodate twenty-five bodies sitting around it—on the floor! The center of the table is decorated with two large bowls of oranges and bananas.

I tiptoe around the narrow border beyond the cloth, taking care not to step on it. This is not easy to do. I go down cross-legged and take off my shoes so they won't go into my plate. I watch others enter, looks of dismay on their faces. So many of our passengers are big—and fat, and old, and handicapped—but somehow they all manage to make it to the floor and sit there looking dazed. Most refuse to eat when the platters of food are unceremoniously dumped on the floor (that is, the "table") before them. Spoons are in short supply—in fact, they are nonexistent until we call for them. (I think we are supposed to eat with our fingers.) The bananas are eaten with relish and we find ourselves playfully tossing them around the room to those who can catch them.

Actually, I discover that the food is very good, once we crawl onto the cloth and dish small samples of the variety on to our plates. There is a meat dish that looks like crumbled hamburger, a potato dish in a tomato sauce, fried eggs on top of a red mixture, and mixed green vegetables of some kind. I find it all good, but most of our group ignore the food entirely except for the bananas. (Some people have even brought a lunch from the ship!) They pass huge rounds of bread as big as pillow cases, which taste about the same, maybe more like a "flannel" cake. One bite of bread is plenty. But the dessert is so good I have two pieces. It is similar to baklava, a thin, dough-like strudel covered with honey. It is served in the same round pie plate that it had been baked in and is cut in wedges. I feel sorry for the people who tried so hard to please us. Most of the food is left on the plates. The food was cooked and I feel it was perfectly safe to eat.

We struggle to our numb feet and arthritic legs after lunch. I stumble down the dark staircase and out into the bright sunlight Men are dancing in the street to the music of traditional instruments—an oud and drums. The dance begins with one man who waves his jimbiya in the air and dances with abandonment. Another man joins the first, and gradually one by one a circle of dancers are hopping around having a great time waving their daggers. One man, very old and very bearded, joins the young men, using his cane to balance himself and to accent the beats, thumping the stones under his feet. No women are seen, but boys and girls hop around the crowd, trying to join in. Everyone is having a good time. At the same time, sales are being made at the small sidewalk shops.

I think it's time to make our way back to the ship, so I climb into our bus Number 1 and soon we are ready to go. Lloyd Tinkle has bought one of the knives complete with a stunning belt. He is pleased with his purchase and I show him mine— a little silver box studded with agates. The lid has an elephant carved in ivory.

We seem to sit for ages waiting for our guide. The driver is in place chewing gat. After forty minutes Roger Ellis, our ship's host on this tour, tells the driver to go. But the driver remonstrates, as he wants to wait for our guide. Roger is angry. "No! We leave now!" Reluctantly the driver pulls away without our guide, leaving him and the other three buses behind.

The gat our driver is chewing is a drug that the Yemenites all chew. They begin after lunch and the stimulant, said our guide, keeps them awake until all hours of the night. Gat is cultivated in fields like marijuana. The leaves are chewed and the stripped stalks are discarded. The floor of the bus around the driver is already littered with stalks, and I can see his face in the rear view mirror. One cheek bulges out like a farmer's cheek full of chewing tobacco. I also notice a large, fresh bunch of gat in the overhead storage. A passenger sitting across from me is chewing too. She confides that the driver offered her some gat, and she accepted. Pretty soon she nods off, so maybe she didn't have enough of it to affect her. Later on I ask what she did with the gat when she stopped chewing it.

"I swallowed it," she said calmly.

The driver wings around the turns and continues to pull off the leaves and tosses the stripped stalks to the floor. Lloyd and I notice that he perspires heavily and constantly mops his face and neck, then reaches for a water bottle for big gulps. By now both cheeks look like a squirrel's storing nuts. We race along the road, taking our half in the middle. Oncoming cars have to give way to us. Fortunately there are not too many cars, so the trip is just slightly hair-raising. I at least have confidence that the driver will not fall asleep at the wheel. With so much gat juice in him he is no doubt riding high.

We arrive at the dock long before the rest of the buses and I thank Roger for his insistence to leave. We suspect that the guides wanted our group to stay as long as possible and clean out the shops. They get a nice commission off the sales, but our guide got no tip from us.

Top: As Queen of the Equator on a 1959 cruise aboard the *Rio de la Plata* (Argentine State Line), Lucina *(second from right)* received royal treatment along with King Neptune and their court of "pirates." *Right:* The "royal family" relaxes on deck during the ceremony.

Lucina (*not shown*) and Sam (*front, with arms crossed*) wait patiently with fellow passengers during a lifeboat drill on the 1959 cruise on the *Rio de la Plata*. Sam's mother (*wearing a scarf*) and stepfather (*in beret*) joined them on this voyage.

Before the handling of koalas was banned, Lucina and Sam had the opportunity to cuddle one of the teddy bear-like marsupials when they visited the wildlife sanctuary in Brisbane, Australia, in 1978.

An Abrupt Halt

April 5

It is Norwegian Day, a special one for our Norwegian ship. The evening is formal and we are welcomed at the skald party preceding dinner, hosted by our captain, Ola S. Harsheim. The entertainment will begin after dinner at ten o'clock. It is the one night on the World Cruise when passengers and crew team up for a program of singing. My stewardess and one of our waiters are in the group, as well as many of our passenger friends. There have been daily rehearsals in the past week, so we look forward to a good concert by the Sailor's Chorus.

I dress in my brown velvet pantsuit, which is warm and comfortable. The ship is always cool with the air conditioning, and I usually wear a jacket in the dining room.

After the captain's dinner, most of the passengers go to the Norway Lounge to see the show. There must be about a hundred performers tonight, half passenger and half crew.

Promptly at ten the passengers in the chorus file onto the stage. The crew is seated in a balcony section adjacent to the stage awaiting their turn.

I have chosen to sit fairly far back in the room where I can see and hear perfectly.

A journalist commented in his article two days later that it was a good thing the first song was not "My Bonnie Lies Over the Ocean," because the group has barely finished their songs and are starting to exchange places with the crew when there's a roll and bump of the ship. The fifty people on stage begin to stagger and topple over, one against the next like a set of dominoes. They all fall down. Startled cries, confusion on stage, and outcries among us in the audience follow. I'm gripping the balcony bench in front of me to keep from rolling over in my chair. What is happening?

The lights go out simultaneously with the engines and we are suddenly in shocked silence. The voice of the captain comes over the loud speaker.

"Our ship has hit something and we are not sure yet what it is. We are taking on water but the watertight doors are keeping the flooded area confined. Everyone please go to your stations on the promenade deck and get life jackets there. Do not go to your cabins—I repeat, do not go to your cabins!"

We quickly and quietly respond to his order and file out of the lounge and down the stairs to deck seven, one deck below. Emergency lights have been turned on, and though they are dim they are adequate. There is no panic and no confusion, but by the time I reach the deck all the life jackets have been taken except for those in a bin of children's sizes. I take one and squeeze it over my head. It's tight but it will do.

The ship begins to list heavily to starboard, and water pours down the dining room windows. The deck is awash. I realize that I should be on the port side where my station is, but I stay put and wait for orders. The life boats are down and ready to board if necessary. One is open directly in front of me. Still dazed and apprehensive, I prefer to stay where I am.

The captain speaks again: "The ship has listed to starboard but we are using the pumps to get her stabilized. Do not leave the deck. Do not use the bathrooms. Crew: Do not go to deck three—stay away from deck three! No one is to go below deck seven."

We are very quiet out on the deck. The sea is calm and the air is warm with a little breeze. All are focused on the situation with one question: What could have happened? Someone has fainted. It is a woman and several people are helping her to lie down.

The captain is on the loud speaker with an update. "The ship is now stabilized, but do not go below deck seven. Stay at your stations on deck."

The officers are now doing a roll call at the stations, so I walk around the ship to my number-ten boat station on the port side and report my presence to the deck officer. This side of the ship is dry and I find a spot where I can sit down on the deck. I'm tired and sleepy and find myself dropping off to sleep. By now it must be after midnight.

A hand jostles my shoulder and I look up to see the ship's doctor bending over me.

"Are you all right?" he asks.

"Sure," I respond. "I'm just trying to get some sleep."

This is only the first time my rest is interrupted. The doctor comes by twice more to check me out as I doze. He has really been taking care of the passengers this night.

The captain keeps us informed every little while. His latest announcement relieves us. "You may all go to the dining room and take off your life jackets, but keep them with you at all times. Do not go below deck seven. Do not go to your cabins. The crew is not allowed on deck three."

People have already opened up deck chairs and are curled up in them, more or less sleeping. Most of us go inside to the dining room to appropriate a table and chairs where we can sit down in relative comfort. I am so sleepy I lean over the table, my head on my arms, to rest even if I can't sleep. Each time I almost doze off the captain comes on with an update.

"The cruise ship *Renaissance V* is approaching our ship on the port side. She will stand by if we need help."

I see the lighted ship. This is the one I was on just two years ago when the stupid captain took us out in a hurricane from the port of Las Palmas in the Canary Islands and we nearly capsized. It was a terrible, frightening night as the small ship fought forty-foot waves and seventy-five mile-an-hour winds. It was an unnecessary exposure to real danger.

We try to get help during the night. At four A.M. an Egyptian tanker comes by on our stern to tow us away from the reef we are drifting towards. A line is thrown to the tanker, but as they begin to tow us, the line snaps. Now we have to wait until morning for tugs to tow us ashore.

By this time I need to find the rest room. It is hard to find a clear path through the dining room as people are sleeping all over the floor. It is hard to see them in the dim light of the emergency lighting and I nearly step on someone. I make my way through the maze of bodies and climb the stair to the eighth deck where the rest rooms are located.

What a shambles the room is in! The toilets are a mess because the water has been shut off all night. The pumps had to be used to keep the water pressure down. There is still some danger that the watertight doors might not hold if the pressure is too great. This is one reason the captain won't allow us in our cabins. Another reason is that there is no electricity in our cabins and the captain doesn't want to add personal injury to the ship's disaster. No one has been hurt and he wants to keep it that way.

By five A.M. I am thoroughly awake and feel restless. My evening clothes are wrinkled and a mess. I am surprised to see that most of my friends have changed their clothes. They have sneaked down to their cabins in spite of the order, and I'm tempted to do the same. The emergency lights are adequate for the hallways and stairs, so I make my way down the two flights to my deck five and let myself in my cabin. I leave the door open to allow a little light to penetrate into the room, but there is also a lightening of the sky outside. I am able to change my clothes at least. Only two glasses from the bar have fallen on the floor and they are not broken. That seems to be the only thing amiss in my cabin. I reach for a life jacket to replace it for the too-small one, but both jackets have been removed from my closet shelf. They must have been collected by the crew in the first stage of our emergency.

I return to the dining room and sit with friends around one of the tables until dawn, and the captain gives us permission to return to our cabins. The dining room needs a cleanup before they can serve us breakfast.

At eight-fifteen we are instructed to start packing. We can take only two bags and one tote with us. Anything more must be left in our cabins and will be shipped to us later. I only have two bags, but I also have two heavy totes and plan to take them anyway. The only problem is the shipping of my pottery elephant, which I bought in Vietnam. Ellen, my stewardess finds a big box for me and some bubblewrap. We pack the elephant and tape the plastic around it, then I fill the box with clothes to pad my five-dollar prize. I hope it will arrive safely.

We have learned that we tore a hole in the hull striking a reef. We were cruising the Red Sea heading for Aqaba in Jordan until we hit the reef. This occurred about fifteen miles off the coast of Sharm al Sheikh in Egypt.

At three-fifteen an announcement from Paul McFarland (cruise director) tells us that we will debark in fifteen minutes. Our baggage lines the hallways, ready for pickup, and I decide to walk slowly with my two heavy totes to the stairway leading down to deck four where we will leave the ship. The stairway and hall are already packed with people. In a few minutes the captain comes on the loud speaker and in an irate voice says, "I don't know how such an announcement to debark happened. We are not ready to leave the ship. The ferry to transport us has not arrived; the thousand pieces of baggage must be loaded first, then the passengers. You will be advised when the time comes. Please stay in your staterooms and wait for the announcement."

I would have been delighted to go back to my cabin and lie down, but when I left it, Ellen the stewardess closed the door and my keys were inside. She disappeared and I have no recourse but to wait it out in the hall. A few stools are brought out and I camp on one of them. No one leaves. We wait like a herd of cattle at the stampede gate for six hours. The bags were all picked up hours ago and we wait momentarily for the announcement that doesn't come until nine P.M. The wait has worn down everyone's nerves—the sleepless night, the strain under the emergency—all go together to drain what is left of our energies.

Finally, when exhaustion is complete we are told it is time. One ferry has filled and will return "later on." I am in the last shipment of cattle, but there is a seat for me on the ferry and I struggle with the too-heavy totes.

The ferry is a catamaran—huge, clean, and very new. We are taken to a dock and spend a lot of time finding our luggage in the dark—the light comes only from the bus headlights waiting to take us to the various hotels in Sharm al Sheikh. When I find my two bags, they are loaded, we are loaded and stuffed into the buses with our totes. It would be a comical sight if we had energy left to laugh.

Fifty-five of us are taken to the Aida Hotel, which is modern and quite beautiful, but there is a hassle at the registration desk about paying for the rooms in advance. They will not accept the ship's voucher. They want cash.

It is one A.M. before they release keys to us. We have been sitting in the lobby like disconsolate zombies for three hours. When they say we can go to our rooms, they also say "please have dinner first. We have it all ready for you out by the pool."

Who wants to eat? We just want to sleep! We walk past the huge buffet and hardly see it on the way to our rooms. I make haste for bed and am out like a light for the next six hours.

In summing up this last experience, I must report that the efforts of the ship's staff and crew could not have been better. Everyone worked tirelessly and around the clock to see to the passengers' needs and welfare. It was a monumental task to arrange hotel space on Easter weekend for over five hundred people, fly us home to our destinations and do it with a red carpet treatment. We stayed in various hotels in Sharm al Sheikh, all of them top-notch establishments. The town of Sharm al Sheikh is really just a resort town, built up and still building, rather like Cancun, Mexico. They have a good beach and have made it popular in just ten years. Before that it was nothing but an expanse of desert.

The Aida Hotel has a lovely pool, shops, excellent food and comfortable rooms. We stayed there for two nights and enjoyed a good folk dance show put on just for us (we were told). On Easter Sunday two chartered 747 Egypt Airline planes flew us to Frankfort or London, depending on our destinations. I was on the plane to London and ticketed in business class. In London we were met by Cunard representatives who handled our baggage and transported us to the Hilton International Hotel at Heathrow Airport. We spent the night there, and at noon on April 8, we flew home via British Airline in business class and it was a marvelous flight, with excellent food and service.

Cunard went all out to give us the best service and accommodations. They paid for everything, including phone calls home and bar drinks. It was all organized within a three-day period and I can't commend highly enough the company and the *Royal Viking Sun* for the swift arrangements made for over five hundred passengers and four hundred crew members. I don't know how they managed it.

The accident has given me even greater confidence in the *Sun*'s Captain Harsheim and his crew. The incident showed how proficiently such an emergency could be handled. I am ready to go again and look forward to the 1997 World Cruise.